VOGUE KNITTING
CAPS&HATS

VOGUE KNITTING
CAPS&HATS

THE BUTTERICK® PUBLISHING COMPANY
NEW YORK

B

THE BUTTERICK® PUBLISHING COMPANY
161 Avenue of the Americas
New York, New York 10013

THE BUTTERICK® PUBLISHING COMPANY and colophon
are registered trademarks of Butterick® Company, Inc.

Manufactured in China

5 7 9 10 8 6

Library of Congress Card Catalog Number: 97-077518

ISBN 1-57389-010-3

First Edition

TABLE OF CONTENTS

INTRODUCTION

How many hats do you wear? Parent, breadwinner, teacher, student, homemaker, spouse, artist, activist—the list is endless; the hours in the day limited. It's a juggling act to get everything done and make time for knitting. But put on your thinking cap and you'll see windows of knitting opportunity around every corner. Your daily commute, a long line at the supermarket, or the sidelines of your daughter's soccer game are perfect moments to get clicking. The projects in the *Knitting on the Go* series are designed for spare minutes. Compact pieces—small in scale, big in creative outlet—that you can take along with you.

Caps and hats top the list for portable projects. They're small enough to slip into your bag, require a minimal investment of time and materials, and offer a wonderful way to explore your creative side. Small projects like these are perfect for trying out new knitting techniques, stitch patterns, and color combinations.

Best of all, hats are fun, practical (who doesn't need a hat?), and expressive. They make great gifts too! The designs on the pages that follow are brimming with personality. The yarns suggested in this book are just a starting point. Pull from your own collection of odds and ends or splurge on a luxury yarn. Experiment with fiber, color and texture (just be sure to make a test swatch for gauge) and create a topper all your own.

Put on your knitting hat, grab your needles and get ready to KNIT ON THE GO!

THE BASICS

For the first-time knitter or the accomplished expert, a hat is one of the simplest and most expressive knitting projects out there. Two or three balls of yarn are all it takes to knit most of the solid color hats in this book, and most can be finished quickly. There's no waste in the styles that are worked in several colors, in most cases the leftover amounts are sufficient for a second hat. The designers who contributed to this book took inspiration from history and world culture to bring you a wealth of styles from which to choose. Whether you knit a hat to express your personality or as a gift for a friend, you're sure to find great pleasure in knitting these projects.

CAP AND HAT CONSTRUCTION

A multitude of hat styles for all levels of experience are featured on the following pages. Novices will appreciate the simple beauty of fast-knitting styles in chunky yarns, while the more experienced will delight in the projects that feature unique shaping and challenging stitch patterns and color combinations.

The easiest styles are knit with fast crown decreases or simple sewn pleats at the top. Some are worked flat on straight needles with a back seam that is sewn invisibly from the right side. Others are worked in the round with a circular needle, switching to double pointed needles as the stitches decrease and no longer fit comfortably on the circulars. Most of the hats in this book are worked by beginning at the lower band or brim edge and continuing up the sides, ending at the crown

center. The most common top finishing is worked after the last round when the stitches are still on the double pointed needles. After cutting the yarn, simply draw it through the remaining stitches at the top twice, pull up firmly, and fasten off. The five-stitch star on the Scottish Tam on page 46 illustrates the beauty of this simple technique. Others use more complex finishing methods described below.

TYPES OF CAPS AND HATS

CAPS

A cap is a snug-fitting hat that fits closely to the head. The finished circumference of these styles will be smaller than your actual head measurement. Caps are also usually worn above or just covering the ears. These simple styles are among the easiest to knit.

Ski and Stocking Caps

Designed for active outdoor wear, especially snow and winter sports, stocking caps have a long pendant tail, often trimmed with a tassel. The Stocking Cap in this book, shown on page 32, features a double-layer pull-out lining as well as a folded brim, which gives extra thickness and warmth. The Tasseled Ski Cap on page 43 is made without any crown decreasing—the top corners are simply tucked inside and sewn down to create the pleated effect at the top. This cap is designed to sit high on the top of the head.

Tams and Berets

Tams and berets are flat caps, often topped with a pom-pom. Most in this book are

GAUGE

It is always important to knit a gauge swatch, and it is even more so with hats as they are designed to fit securely. If your gauge is too loose, you could end up with your hat over your eyes, if it's too tight, the hat will perch oddly at the top of your head.

Making a flat gauge swatch for hats knit in the round will allow you to measure gauge over a 4"/10cm span that will lay flat for better reading. However, when a hat includes a complex stitch pattern knit in rounds, a circularly-knit swatch will test the gauge best and the practice will familiarize you with the pattern—cast on at least as many stitches required for the hat. The type of needles used—straight or double pointed, wood or metal—will influence gauge, so knit your swatch with the needles you plan to use for the project. Measure gauge as illustrated. Try different needle sizes until your sample measures the required number of stitches and rows. To get fewer stitches to the inch/cm, use larger needles; to get more stitches to the inch/cm, use smaller needles.

Knitting in the round may tighten the gauge, so if you measured the gauge on a flat swatch, take another gauge reading after you begin your hat. When the hat measures at least 2"/5cm, lay it flat and measure over the stitches in the center of the piece, as the side stitches may be distorted. Keep in mind that if you consciously try to loosen your tension to match the flat knit swatch you can prevent having to go up a needle size.

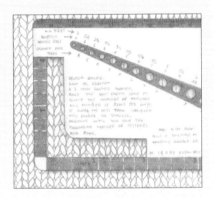

worked beginning at the band edges in a close-fitting rib pattern or finished with ribbon or elastic. Since the tam and beret style only has to fit the head around the band edge, the band is usually elastic enough to fit all sizes. When the band is completed, several stitches are increased in one or two rows or rounds. After several inches, decreases are worked at even intervals to form the signature flat shape. Decorative decreases that form the

pie-shaped wedges defining the beret crown are a special feature of the style.

The one exception to this formula for crown decreasing is the Cabled Beret on page 27. Here, the stitch pattern is worked in a long strip to fit fully around the head circumference. Stitches are picked up along the side of one long edge and the band is worked downwards. Then, using a tapestry needle, the remaining long edge is gathered along the sides of the cable rows to form a flat crown. The accordion nature of the stitch pattern makes this technique possible. In a different stitch pattern, this method would be too bulky.

HATS

Hats are more structured than caps and usually consist of a crown and a brim. Worn since the 10th century, early hats were designed to signify the importance of the wearer. These styles often require more shaping than caps and are both a challenge and fun to knit.

Brimmed Hats

These styles flatter the face and exude an air of sophistication, and they are influenced by traditional millinery techniques. The Woolly Derby on page 50 is a loose-fitting style in a lightweight yarn that will fit a range of sizes comfortably. The double-knit stitch and resilient yarn used for the Cloche Hat on page 64 results in an elastic fit. Both styles have convertible turn up or down brims. The Summer Straw Hat on page 67 is worked in raffia then dipped in a basin of undiluted starch to give it structure. While the hat is still wet, it is shaped over a head form, with the brim in a flattened position. (More on this blocking method on page 69.) The brim of the Fisherman's Hat on page 80 is faced with fusible webbing and fabric, then top stitched.

With its faced band and hidden purl increases along the sides, the Cabled Hat on page 76 takes on the dimension of a crown. This is the only hat with a crown that begins at the center top. The stitches are worked outwards to form a circle, a technique that makes the hat crown lie flatter.

SIZING

Most of the hats and caps in this book are sized for women. Those suitable for men and children are indicated in the sizes section of the instructions.

To avoid making a hat that is too tight, measure for head size before you begin to knit. Sizing is particularly important for structured hat styles. To measure, place a tape measure across the forehead and measure around the full circumference of the head. Keep the tape snug for accurate results.

Head sizes used in this book		
SIZE	INCHES	CM
X-Small	20	51
Small	21	53
Medium	22	56
Large	23	59

Helmets, Toques and Pillboxes

These styles sport flat or slightly rounded tops with straight sides. They sit fairly high on the head and utilize a special millinery-inspired rolled trim. The flat tops are achieved by decreases worked in slanting or spiral patterns.

YARN SELECTION

For an exact reproduction of the hats photographed, use the yarn listed in the materials section of the pattern. We've chosen yarns that are readily available in the U.S. and Canada at the time of printing. The Resources list on pages 94 and 95 provides addresses of yarn distributors. Contact them for the name of a retailer in your area.

YARN SUBSTITUTION

You may wish to substitute yarns. Perhaps you view small-scale projects as a chance to incorporate leftovers from your yarn stash, or the yarn specified may not be available in your area. You'll need to knit to the given gauge to obtain the knitted measurements with a substitute yarn (see "Gauge" on page 11). Be sure to consider how the fiber content of the substitute yarn will affect the comfort and the ease of care of your hats.

To facilitate yarn substitution, *Vogue Knitting* grades yarn by the standard stitch gauge obtained in Stockinette stitch. You'll find a grading number in the "Materials" section of the pattern, immediately following the fiber type of the yarn. Look for a substitute yarn that falls into the same category. The suggested gauge on the ball band should be comparable to that on the Yarn Symbols chart (see page 14).

After you've successfully gauge-swatched a substitute yarn, you'll need to figure out how much of the substitute yarn the project requires. First, find the total length of the original yarn in the pattern (multiply number of balls by yards/meters per ball). Divide this figure by the new yards/meters per ball (listed on the ball band). Round up to the next whole number. The answer is the number of balls required.

FOLLOWING CHARTS

Charts are a convenient way to follow colorwork, lace, cable and other stitch patterns at a glance. *Vogue Knitting* stitch charts utilize the universal knitting language of "symbolcraft." When knitting in the round, read charts from right to left on every round, repeating any stitch and row repeats as directed in the pattern. When knitting back and forth in rows, read charts from right to left on right side (RS) rows and from left to right on wrong side (WS) rows. Posting a self-adhesive note under your working row is an easy way to keep track of your place on a chart.

COLORWORK KNITTING

Two main types of colorwork are explored in this book.

Intarsia

Intarsia is accomplished with separate bobbins of individual colors. This method is ideal for large blocks of color or for motifs that aren't repeated close together, such as the Harlequin Beret on page 70. When changing colors, always pick up the new color and wrap it around the old color to prevent holes.

Stranding

When motifs are closely placed, colorwork is accomplished by stranding along two or more colors per row, creating "floats" on the wrong side of the fabric. This technique is sometimes called Fair Isle knitting, after the traditional Fair Isle patterns composed of small motifs with frequent color changes.

BLOCKING

Blocking is an all-important finishing step in the knitting process. Most hats retain their shape after pressing if the blocking stages in the instructions are followed carefully. (The one exception is the Summer Straw Hat on page 67, which will lose its shape when wet.) If you plan to make several hats, invest in a head form. They can be purchased from mail-order sources and are made of wood, wire or Styrofoam. If you don't have a headform, an inverted bowl will make a reasonable substitute.

Wet Block Method

Place the hat on a head form and lightly dampen using a spray bottle. Allow to dry before removing.

To achieve a flat crisp edge on tams and berets, wet the knitted piece and insert a dinner plate (of appropriate size). Leave the hat to dry (with the plate in place) on a towel.

Steam Block Method

Using a head form or plate as described, steam lightly using a steam iron or steamer approximately 2"/5cm above the knitting. Do not press or it will flatten the stitches.

FINISHING TECHNIQUES

Several embellishments are used to trim the hats in this book, such as pom-poms and tassels. Most hats are very simply finished at the crown by drawing a long end through the last stitches on the needles. When a hat is knit flat, an invisible back seam should be sewn from the right side.

YARN SYMBOLS

① **Fine Weight**
(29-32 stitches per 4"/10cm)
Includes baby and fingering yarns, and some of the heavier crochet cottons. The range of needle sizes is 0-4 (2-3.5mm).

② **Lightweight**
(25-28 stitches per 4"/10cm)
Includes sport yarn, sock yarn, UK 4-ply and lightweight DK yarns. The range of needle sizes is 3-6 (3-4mm).

③ **Medium Weight**
(21-24 stitches per 4"/10cm)
Includes DK and worsted, the most commonly used knitting yarns. The range of needle sizes is 6-9 (4-5.5mm).

④ **Medium-heavy Weight**
(17-20 stitches per 4"/10cm)
Also called heavy worsted or Aran. The range of needle sizes is 8-10 (5-6mm).

⑤ **Bulky Weight**
(13-16 stitches per 4"/10cm)
Also called chunky. Includes heavier Icelandic yarns. The range of needle sizes is 10-11 (6-8mm).

⑥ **Extra-bulky Weight**
(9-12 stitches per 4"/10cm)
The heaviest yarns available. The range of needle sizes is 11 and up (8mm and up).

CIRCULAR NEEDLES

Hold the needle tip with the last cast-on stitch in your right hand and the tip with the first cast-on stitch in your left hand. Knit the first cast-on stitch, pulling the yarn tight to avoid a gap.

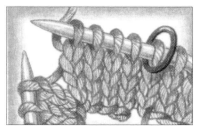

Work until you reach the marker. This completes the first round. Slip the marker to the right needle and work the next round.

TWISTED CORD

1 If you have someone to help you, insert a pencil or knitting needle through each end of the strands. If not, place one end over a doorknob and put a pencil through the other end. Turn the strands clockwise until they are tightly twisted.

2 Keeping the strands taut, fold the piece in half. Remove the pencils and allow the cords to twist onto themselves.

DOUBLE POINTED NEEDLES

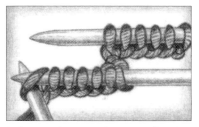

1 Cast on the required number of stitches on the first needle, plus one extra. Slip this extra stitch to the next needle as shown. Continue in this way, casting on the required number of stitches on the last needle.

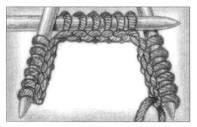

2 Arrange the needles as shown, with the cast-on edge facing the center of the triangle (or square).

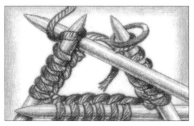

3 Place a stitch marker after the last cast-on stitch. With the free needle, knit the first cast-on stitch, pulling the yarn tightly. Continue knitting in rounds, slipping the marker before beginning each round.

TASSELS

Cut a piece of cardboard to the desired length of the tassel. Wrap yarn around the cardboard. Knot a piece of yarn tightly around one end, cut as shown, and remove the cardboard. Wrap and tie yarn around the tassel about 1"/2.5cm down from the top to secure the fringe.

POM-POMS

1 Following the template, cut two circular pieces of cardboard.

2 Hold the two circles together and wrap the yarn tightly around the cardboard several times. Secure and carefully cut the yarn.

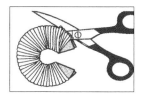

3 Tie a piece a yarn tightly between the two circles. Remove the cardboard and trim the pom-pom to the desired size.

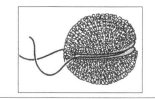

TO BEGIN SEAMING

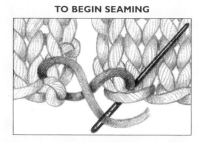

If you have left a long tail from your cast-on row, you can use this strand to begin sewing. To make a neat join at the lower edge with no gap, use the technique shown here. Thread the strand into a yarn needle. With the rights sides of both pieces facing you, insert the yarn needle from back to front into the corner stitch of the piece without the tail. Making a figure eight with the yarn, insert the needle from back to front into the stitch with the cast-on tail. Tighten to close the gap.

INVISIBLE SEAMING: STOCKINETTE ST

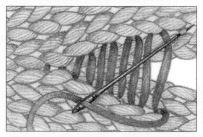

Insert the needle under the horizontal bar between the first and second stitches. Insert the needle into the corresponding bar on the other piece. Continue alternating from side to side.

POM-POM TEMPLATES

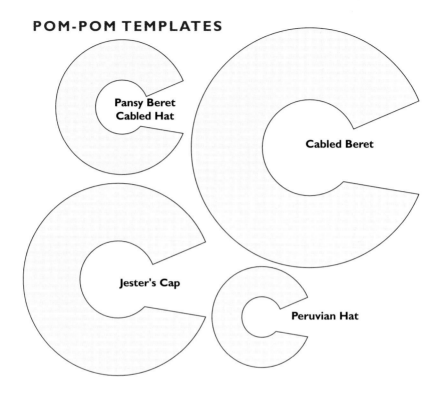

**Pansy Beret
Cabled Hat**

Cabled Beret

Jester's Cap

Peruvian Hat

THREADING BEADS

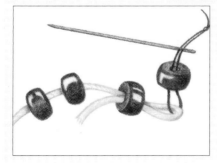

Thread beads onto balls of yarn before you knit. The threading needle must be large enough to accommodate the yarn, but small enough to go through the beads. Since this combination is not always possible, you can use an auxiliary thread to thread the beads. Using a sturdy thread, loop it through a folded piece of yarn and then pull both ends of the thread through the eye of the needle. Pass the bead over the needle and thread it onto the yarn. (It may help to pass a bead back and forth over the folded yarn a few times to crease it.)

KNITTING TERMS AND ABBREVIATIONS

approx approximately

beg begin(ning)

bind off Used to finish an edge and keep stitches from unraveling. Lift the first stitch over the second, the second over the third, etc. (UK: cast off)

cast on A foundation row of stitches placed on the needle in order to begin knitting.

CC contrast color

ch chain(s)

cm centimeter(s)

cont continu(e)(ing)

dc double crochet (UK: tr-treble)

dec decrease(ing)-Reduce the stitches in a row (knit 2 together).

dpn double pointed needle(s)

foll follow(s)(ing)

g gram(s)

garter stitch Knit every row. Circular knitting: knit one round, then purl one round.

hdc half double crochet (UK: htr-half treble)

inc increase(ing)-Add stitches in a row (knit into the front and back of a stitch).

k knit

k2tog knit 2 stitches together

LH left-hand

lp(s) loops(s)

m meter(s)

M I make one stitch-With the needle tip, lift the strand between last stitch worked and next stitch on the left-hand needle and knit into the back of it. One stitch has been added.

MC main color

mm millimeter(s)

no stitch On some charts, "no stitch" is indicated with shaded spaces where stitches have been decreased or not yet made. In such cases, work the stitches of the chart, skipping over the "no stitch" spaces.

oz ounce(s)

p purl

p2tog purl 2 stitches together

pat(s) pattern

pick up and knit (purl) Knit (or purl) into the loops along an edge.

pm place markers-Place or attach a loop of contrast yarn or purchased stitch marker as indicated.

psso pass slip stitch(es) over

rem remain(s)(ing)

rep repeat

rev St st reverse Stockinette stitch-Purl right-side rows, knit wrong-side rows. Circular knitting: purl all rounds. (UK: reverse stocking stitch)

rnd(s) round(s)

RH right-hand

RS right side(s)

sc single crochet (UK: dc—double crochet)

sk skip

SKP Slip 1, knit 1, pass slip stitch over knit 1.

SK2P Slip 1, knit 2 together, pass slip stitch over the knit 2 together.

sl slip-An unworked stitch made by passing a stitch from the left-hand to the right-hand needle as if to purl.

sl st slip stitch (UK: single crochet)

ssk slip, slip, knit - Slip next 2 stitches knitwise, one at a time, to right-hand needle.

Insert tip of left-hand needle into fronts of these stitches from left to right. Knit them together. One stitch has been decreased.

sssk Slip next 3 sts knitwise, one at a time, to right-hand needle. Insert tip of left-hand needle into fronts of these stitches from left to right. Knit them together. Two stitches have been decreased.

st(s) stitch(es)

St st Stockinette stitch-Knit right-side rows, purl wrong-side rows. Circular knitting: knit all rounds. (UK: stocking stitch)

tbl through back of loop

tog together

WS wrong side(s)

wyib with yarn in back

wyif with yarn in front

work even Continue in pattern without increasing or decreasing. (UK: work straight)

yd yard(s)

yo yarn over-Make a new stitch by wrapping the yarn over the right-hand needle. (UK: yfwd, yon, yrn)

* = repeat directions following * as many times as indicated.

[ ] = Repeat directions inside brackets as many times as indicated.

CROCHET STITCHES

CHAIN

1 Pass the yarn over the hook and catch it with the hook.

2 Draw the yarn through the loop on the hook.

3 Repeat steps 1 and 2 to make a chain.

SINGLE CROCHET

1 Insert the hook through top two loops of a stitch. Pass the yarn over the hook and draw up a loop—two loops on hook.

2 Pass the yarn over the hook and draw through both loops on hook.

3 Continue in the same way, inserting the hook into each stitch.

SWIRL CAP

Up in a cloud of smoke

Decorative dimensional swirls, worked in stepped spiral decreases, converge into a knotted I-cord atop this close-fitting cap. Designed by Norah Gaughan.

SIZE
One size fits all.

KNITTED MEASUREMENTS
■ Head circumference 19½"/50cm
■ Depth 7½"/19cm

MATERIALS
■ 2 1¾oz/50g balls (each approx 143yd/134m) of Grignasco/JCA *Diamante* (wool/cashmere③) in #447 wedgewood blue
■ One each sizes 3 and 5 (3 and 3.75mm) circular needles, 16"/40cm long *or size to obtain gauge*
■ One set (4) size 5 (3.75mm) dpn
■ Cable needle (cn)
■ Stitch markers

GAUGE
24 sts and 32 rows to 4"/10cm over chart pat using size 5 (3.75mm) needles.
Take time to check gauge

CAP
Beg at lower edge, with smaller circular needle, cast on 116 sts. Join, taking care not to twist sts on needle. Mark end of rnd and sl marker every rnd. Work in k2, p2 rib for ¾"/2cm. Change to larger circular needle and k 1 rnd, dec 1 st at beg—115 sts.

Beg cable chart pat
Rnd 1 Foll chart, work 23-st rep of rnd 1 5 times—140 sts.
Rnds 2-11 Foll chart, work 28-st rep 5 times.
Rnds 12-22 Foll chart, work 30-st rep 5 times.
Rnds 23-38 Foll chart, work 25-st rep 5 times.
Rnds 39-42 Foll chart, dec as indicated.
Rnd 43 Foll chart, working 23-st rep 4 times, then on the 5th rep, work to last 4 sts of rnd, place new marker, work to end, remove old marker—110 sts. Change to dpn and cont to foll chart rnds 44-50—20 sts rem. K 1 rnd on all sts.
Next rnd [K2tog] 10 times.
Next rnd [K2tog] 4 times—6 sts rem. Cont to work even on 6 sts until "cord" at top measures 3"/7.5cm. Bind off. Pull end through bound-off sts to close. Tie cord into a knot. Block finished piece lightly.

M3

K 1 st into front, back and front of st to make 3 sts.

M6

[K into front and back of st] 3 times to make 6 sts.

Dec 5

[K3tog]twice, pass first st over 2nd st to make 1 st from 6.

3-ST LPC

Sl 2 sts to cn and hold to *front*, p1, k2 from cn.

4-ST RC

Sl 2 sts to cn and hold to *back*, k2, k2 from cn.

4-ST RPC

Sl 1 st to cn and hold to *back*, k3, p1 from cn.

4-ST LPC

Sl 3 sts to cn and hold to *front*, p1, k3 from cn.

2/2-ST LPC

Sl 2 sts to cn and hold to *front*, p2, k2 from cn.

4 to 3-ST RPC

Sl 2 sts to cn and hold to *back*, k2, p2tog from cn.

5-ST RC

Sl 2 sts to cn and hold to *back*, k3, k2 from cn.

5-ST RPC

Sl 2 sts to cn and hold to *back*, k3, p2 from cn.

5-ST LPC

Sl 3 sts to cn and hold to *front*, p2, k3 from cn.

6-ST RC

Sl 3 sts to cn and hold to *back*, k3, k3 from cn.

6-ST LC

Sl 3 sts to cn and hold to *front*, k3, k3 from cn.

6-ST RPC

Sl 3 sts to cn and hold to *back*, k3, p3 from cn.

6-ST LPC

Sl 3 sts to cn and hold to *front*, p3, k3 from cn.

Stitch key

- k on RS, p on WS
- p on RS, k on WS
- No stitch
- M1
- M3
- 6 M6
- p2 tog
- k2tog
- k3tog
- 5 dec 5
- 3-st LPC
- 4-st RC
- 4-st RPC
- 4-st LPC
- 2/2-st LPC
- 4 to 3-st RPC
- 5-st RC
- 5-st RPC
- 5-st LPC
- 6-st RC
- 6-st LC
- 6-st RPC
- 6-st LPC

CABLE CHART

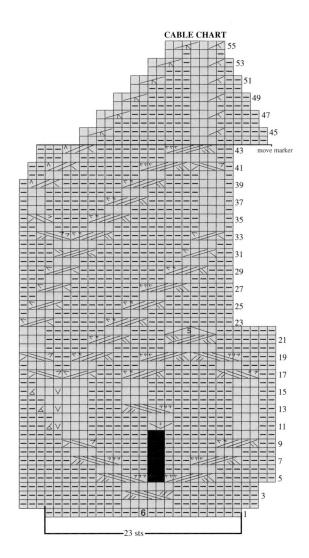

move marker

23 sts

Knit-in beads add new dimension to the pillbox, a '60s wardrobe staple. Designed by Nadia Severns, it features a criss-crossed rolled band, beaded crown decreases, and an elaborate tassel.

SIZES
One size fits all.

KNITTED MEASUREMENTS
- Head circumference 22"/56cm
- Depth 7"/18cm

MATERIALS
- 2 1¾oz/50g hanks (each approx 176yd/162m) of Koigu Wool Designs *Premium Merino* (wool②) in #2380 copper (MC)
- 1 1¾oz/50g hanks (each approx 176yd/162m) of Koigu Wool Designs *Painters Palette Premium Merino* (wool②) in #P508 multi (CC)
- One each sizes 1 and 3 (2.25 and 3mm) circular needles, 16"/40cm long *or size to obtain gauge*
- One set (5) size 3 (3mm) dpn
- Approx 600 assorted beads, a mix of triangle beads and sizes 5 and 6 seed beads in assorted colors and matte/shiny finishes. (Beads by Caravan Beads, see US Resources on page 94.)
- Two each ⅝"/15mm flat teardrop beads in matte metallic copper and ⅜"/10mm faceted matte amber tubular beads
- One ¾"/20mm faced gold metallic bicone bead, for crown center
- Large-eye needle and thread for threading beads onto yarn

GAUGE
28 sts and 36 rows to 4"/10cm in St st using larger needles.

Take time to check gauge.

Notes on bead knitting
Thread beads in random colors onto yarn before beg to knit beaded section. Approx 416 beads are required for the beaded hat side section, but thread several more to ensure an exact number. Work one rnd in plain St st (k 1 st as you normally would knit). The second rnd, which is the beaded rnd, is worked in "Eastern Cross" knitting, to slant in the opposite direction and to prevent beaded section from having a bias.

HAT
Beg at lower edge with smaller circular needle and unbeaded ball of MC, cast on 124 sts. Join, taking care not to twist sts on needle. Mark end of rnd and sl marker every rnd. K 8 rnds for rolled hem. Then work in k1, p1 rib for 8 rnds. Change to larger circular needle and k 1 rnd, inc 32 sts evenly spaced—156 sts. K 1 rnd. Cut yarn. Attach beaded ball of yarn.

Rnd 1 (beaded rnd) *[Insert RH needle into the back of st and wrap yarn away from you and around needle (instead of wrapping the yarn towards you as with plain St st) and k1 st as in "Eastern Cross" knitting] 3 times (for 3 "Eastern-Cross" sts), then as the yarn is wrapped, slide a bead towards the next st and push it through the st with the wrap just before slipping st off needle (for 1 beaded st), work 2 more "Eastern-Cross" sts; rep from * (for 6-st rep) 25 more times around.

Rnd 2 Knit (the usual way).

Rnd 3 *Work 1 beaded st, work 5 "Eastern Cross" sts; rep from * 25 more times around.

Rnd 4 Knit (the usual way).

Rep rnds 1-4 for beaded pat until there are 32 rnds from beg and piece measures approx 4"/10cm with edge rolled.

Braided edge

Rnd I *K1 MC, k1 CC; rep from * around.

Rnd 2 Bring both colors to RS of work and always bringing new color up from over the old color, *p1 MC, p1 CC; rep from * around (colors will twist on this rnd and untwist on the foll rnd).

Rnd 3 *P1 MC, p1 CC; rep from * around always bringing up new color from under the old color. Return yarn to WS of work, cut CC. K 1 rnd with MC. Cut yarn.

Crown

Thread 96 beads onto yarn (plus several extra) to work crown pat. Change to dpn on crown when there are too few sts to fit onto circular needle.

Rnd I *With MC, k25, work 1 "Eastern-Cross" beaded st; rep from * 5 times more.

Rnd 2 Knit all sts (the usual way).

Rnd 3 Rep rnd 1.

Dec rnd 4 *K2tog, k21, ssk, k beaded st; rep from * 5 times more—144 sts.

Rnds 5 and 7 *K 23, work 1 "Eastern-Cross" beaded st; rep from * 5 times more.

Rnd 6 Knit all sts (the usual way).

Rnd 8 *K2tog, k to last 2 sts before bead, ssk, k beaded st; rep from * 5 times more—132 sts.

Rnd 9 Knit all sts (the usual way).

Rnds 10-27 Rep these 2 rnds 9 times more—24 sts.

Rnd 28 *K3tog, k beaded st; rep from * 5 times more—12 sts.

Rnd 29 Knit. Draw yarn through sts on needle twice and fasten. Leave long end for stringing tassel.

FINISHING

Wet block hat using a size medium head form (see "The Basics" page 10). Allow hat to dry completely. With CC, work long cross sts over rolled lower edge to hold in place. Sew large teardrop bead at center front. String 9 beads onto two threads and sew each string looped over ribbed band either side of center front bead. String 3 lengths of beads (one 25 beads, one 37 beads and one 45 beads in length) adding bicone beads at center and at tassel ends as shown in photo on page 24.

CABLED BERET

Accordion pleats

Deeply-textured cabled beret is knit in a straight strip. As the crown gathers at the center, the rows of the stitch pattern naturally form accordion pleats.

SIZES
One size fits all.

KNITTED MEASUREMENTS
- Head circumference 22"/56cm
- Diameter 9½"/24cm

MATERIALS
- 3 1¾oz/50g skeins (each approx 107yd/98m) of Lion Brand *AL•PA•KA* (acrylic/wool/alpaca⑤) in #098 natural
- One pair each sizes 4, 5 and 7 (3.5, 3.75 and 4.5mm) needles *or size to obtain gauge*
- Cable needle (cn)
- Tapestry needle

GAUGE
25 sts and 30 rows to 4"/10cm over cabled pat st using size 7 (4.5mm) needles.
Take time to check gauge.

Note Beret is constructed by first working a straight strip. Then sts are picked up along one long edge of strip to work ribbed band downwards. Then back seam is sewn and sts along other edge are gathered tog to form crown center.

CABLED PATTERN STITCH
Multiple of 8 sts plus 4.
Row I and all WS rows K2, p to last 2 sts, k2.
Rows 2, 4, 8 and 10 Knit.
Row 6 K2, *sl 4 sts to cn and hold to *back*, k4, k4 from cn; rep from *, end k2.
Row 12 K6, *sl 4 sts to cn and hold to *front*, k4, k4 from cn; rep from *, end k6.
Rep rows 1-12 for cabled pat st.

BERET
With size 7 (4.5mm) needles, cast on 52 sts. Work 12 rows of cable pat st 14 times and piece measures approx 22½"/57cm from beg. Bind off.

Ribbed band
With size 5 (3.75mm) needles, pick up and k 106 sts evenly spaced along one long edge of cabled strip.
Row I (RS) K1 (selvage st), *k2, p2; rep from *, end k1 (selvage st). Cont in k2, p2 rib as established for a total of 1"/2.5cm. Change to size 4 (3.5mm) needles and cont in rib for 1"/2.5cm more. Bind off in rib.

FINISHING
Block piece lightly. Sew short edges tog to form back seam. Working along other long end of strip, with tapestry needle, draw through 1 st at end of every other row and pull up tightly to form center of crown. Leave end for attaching pom-pom. Make a 2½"/6.5cm pom-pom and attach to center of crown.

OVERSIZED CABLED HAT

Headwear with an urban edge

Chunky stitching is quick to knit with two strands of bulky yarn. Oversized cables and ribbed topper add downtown drama. Designed by Jacquelyn Smyth.

SIZES
One size fits all.

KNITTED MEASUREMENTS
- Head circumference 23"/59cm
- Depth 13"/33cm

MATERIALS
- 6 1¾oz/50g balls (each approx 39yd/35m) of Filatura Di Crosa/Stacy Charles *Muschio* (alpaca/wool/acrylic/polyamide⑤) in #353 lt brown
- Size 15 (10mm) circular needle, 16"/40cm long *or size to obtain gauge*
- 1 set (4) size 15 (10mm) dpn
- Stitch marker
- Cable needle (cn)
- Matching thread

GAUGE
7 sts and 8 rows to 4"/10cm over rev St st and cable pat using yarn doubled and size 15 (10mm) needles.
Take time to check gauge.

Note Use two strands of yarn held tog throughout.

HAT
Beg at lower edge with double stand of yarn and circular needle, cast on 45 sts. Join, taking care not to twist sts on needle. Mark end of rnd and sl marker every rnd. Work in rnds as foll:
Rnd 1 *K6, p3; rep from * around.
Rnds 2-4 Rep rnd 1.

Rnd 5 *Sl next 3 sts to cn and hold to *back*, k3, k3 from cn, p3; rep from * around.
Rnds 6-12 Rep rnd 1.
Rnd 13 Rep rnd 5.
Rnds 14-16 Rep rnd 1. Bind off.

CROWN
With RS facing, double strand of yarn and dpn, pick up and k 40 sts from bound-off edge picking up behind the bound-off loops. (Bound-off edge forms a chain-loop edge on RS, see photo.) Join, pm at beg of rnd and work in rnds as foll:
Rnd 1 *K2tog, [p1, k1] 4 times, p2tog, [k1, p1] 4 times; rep from * once—36 sts.
Rnds 2 and 3 Work even in k1, p1 rib.
Rnd 4 [P2tog] 6 times, [p2tog, p1] 8 times—22 sts.
Rnds 5-9 Work even in k1, p1 rib. Cut yarn, leaving long end for sewing. Pull through sts on needles and draw up tightly. Pull gathered top to inside to form slight indent at top.

FINISHING
Block lightly to measurements. Fold first 2 rnds of hat to WS and sew in place with thread to give firmness to lower edge. Take single strand of yarn and draw through sts on rnd 4 (p rnd) at top. Gather slightly to form top knot as in photo. Fasten off.

STOCKING CAP

Nordic nightcap

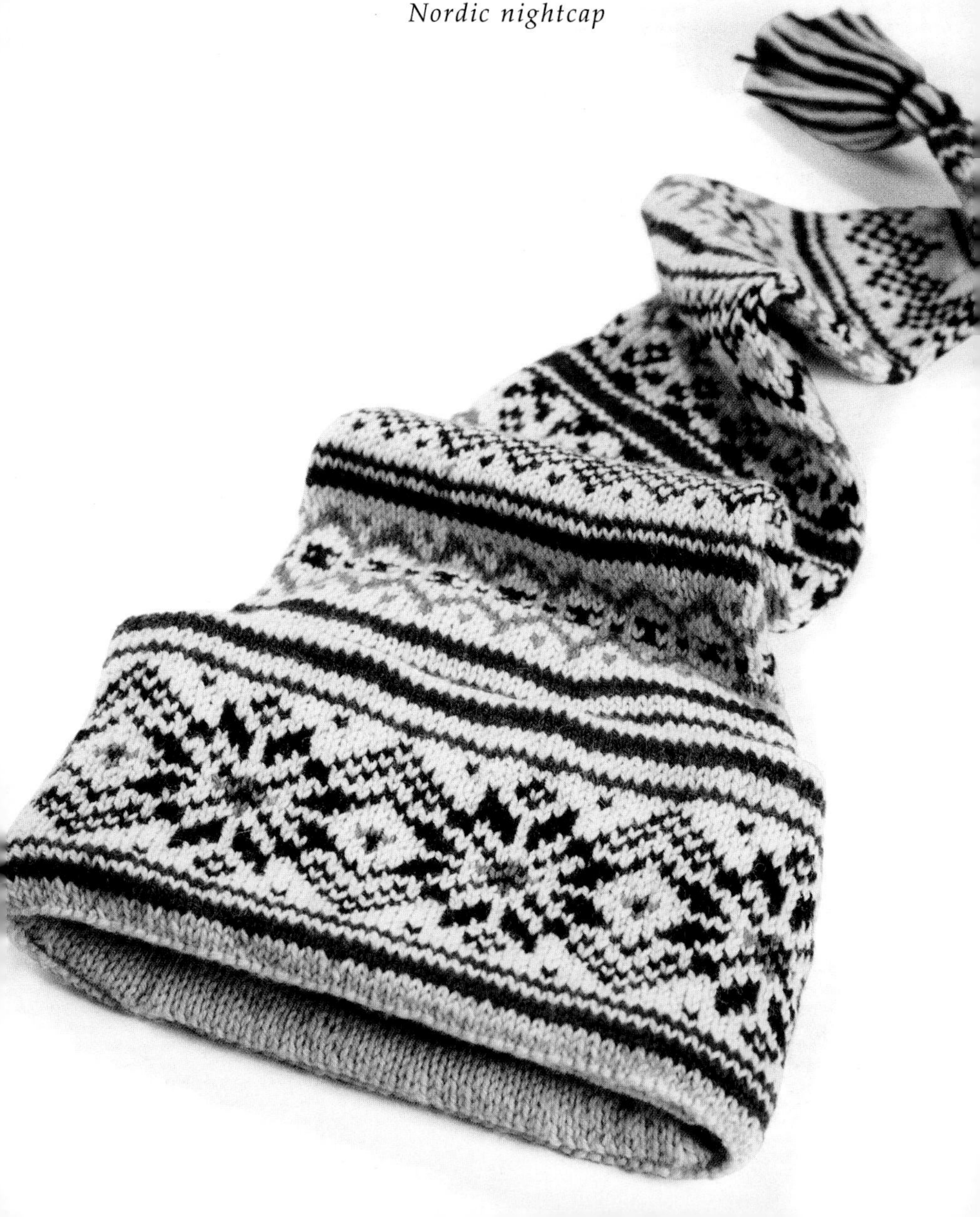

For Intermediate Knitters

To save colored yarn, thrifty Swedish knitters traditionally used a single color to line a "dubblemosa" stocking cap. Diane Zangl's version is decorated with Scandinavian motifs; a pull-out lining forms the inside, keeping heads doubly warm.

SIZES

Instructions are written for Unisex size Small/Medium (21-22"/51-53cm). Changes for size Large/X-Large (23-24"/59-61cm) are in parentheses. Shown in size Small/Medium.

KNITTED MEASUREMENTS

■ Head circumference 20 (23½)"/51 (59.5)cm
■ Depth (excluding stocking top) 8"/20.5cm
■ Length (including stocking top) 27"/68.5cm

MATERIALS

■ 5 (6) 1¾oz/50g balls (each approx 116yd/106m) of Dale of Norway *Falk* (wool③) in #0020 natural (MC)
■ 1 ball each in #5943 pale blue (A), #5744 med blue (B) and #5563 navy (C)
■ One each sizes 3 and 4 (3 and 3.5mm) circular needles, 16"/40cm long *or size to obtain gauge*
■ 1 set (5) each sizes 3 and 4 (3 and 3.5mm) dpn
■ Stitch markers

GAUGE

24 sts and 28 rows to 4"/10cm over St st and chart pat using larger needles.
Take time to check gauge.

Note When changing colors, twist yarns tog on WS to prevent holes. Carry yarn not in use loosely at back of work.

CAP

Brim

With larger circular needle and MC, cast on 120 (140) sts. Join, taking care not to twist sts on needle. Mark end of rnd and sl marker every rnd. P 1 rnd, k 2 rnds.

Beg chart I

Next rnd Work 20-st rep 6 (7) times. Cont to foll chart through rnd 32.

Outer lining

Change to MC and work even with MC in St st until piece measures 8"/20.5cm from beg.

Next (dec) rnd Dec 6 sts evenly spaced around—114 (134) sts. Work even until piece measures 12"/30.5cm from beg.

Next (dec) rnd Dec 6 sts evenly spaced around—108 (128) sts. Work even until piece measures 16"/40.5cm from beg.

Next (dec) rnd Dec 6 sts evenly spaced around—102 (122) sts. Work even until piece measures 16½"/42cm from beg.

Stocking top

Note Change to dpn when there are too few sts to fit on circular needle.

Beg chart II

Dec 6 (8) sts evenly spaced on first rnd (see * on chart). Cont to dec 6 sts on each rnd marked with a * as foll: rnds 1, 5, 22, 28, 57 and 62, AT SAME TIME, foll chart II rnds 1-90 once, rnds 1-37 once, k 2 rnds MC, work chart rnds 56-62 once, 70-75 once and 56-62 once. After all decs there are 18 (36) sts.

Next (dec) rnd [K2tog] 9 (18) times. Work 0 (1) rnd even.

Next (dec) rnd *For Large size only,* [k2tog] 9 times—9 sts rem for both sizes. Cut yarn and pull through sts on needles twice and draw up tightly to fasten. Secure end inside.

Inner lining

With RS facing, smaller circular needle and MC, pick up and k 1 st in each st along cast-on edge—120 (140) sts. Join, place marker for end of rnd.

Rnd 1 Knit, dec 12 (14) sts evenly spaced around—108 (126) sts. Work even in St st with MC until lining measures 7 (8)"/17.5 (20.5)cm

Top shaping

Note Change to dpn when there are too few sts to fit on needle.

Next rnd [K7, k2tog] 12 (14) times—96 (112) sts. K 1 rnd.

Next rnd [K6, k2tog] 12 (14) times—84 (98) sts. K 1 rnd. Cont to dec in this way every other rnd, having 1 less st before each dec on each dec rnd until 12 (14) sts rem. Cut yarn and pull through sts on needles twice and draw up tightly to fasten. Secure end inside.

FINISHING

Block cap to measurements. Make a 4½"/11.5cm tassel with all colors and attach to end of stocking cap. Fold cap at turning ridge of brim and push lining to inside. Fold brim again at 2 MC rows above chart brim and steam flat. With MC, tack folded brim to 2 rows below stocking cap (chart II) at 3"/7.5cm intervals around.

CHART II

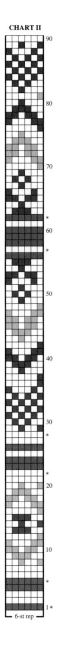

Color key

☐ Natural (MC)

▨ Pale Blue (A)

▨ Medium Blue (B)

■ Navy (C)

* Dec Rnd

CHART I

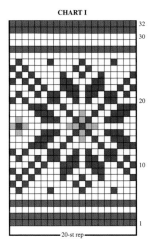

— 20-st rep —

PERUVIAN CAP

An Andean adventure

Based on the ch'ullu design worn by men in Peru and Bolivia, Pam Allen's design features multiple stitches and color artistry. Tiny pom-poms trim curved earflaps; a picot edge frames it all.

SIZES

Instructions are written for Woman's size Small/Medium (21-22"/53-56cm). Changes for size Large (23"/59cm) are in parentheses. Shown in size Small/Medium.

KNITTED MEASUREMENTS

▪ Head circumference 20½ (21½)"/52 (54.5)cm
▪ Depth 7½"/19cm

MATERIALS

▪ 1 3½oz/100g skein each (each approx 183yd/167m) of Tahki Imports *Donegal Tweed* (wool④) in #893 orange (A), #836 purple (B), #861 teal (C), #863 red (D), #803 lime (E) and #882 blue (F)
▪ Size 8 (5mm) circular needle, 16"/40cm long *or size to obtain gauge*
▪ 1 set (4) size 8 (5mm) dpn
▪ Size G/6 (4.5mm) crochet hook

GAUGE

18 sts and 30 rows to 4"/10cm over pat st foll chart using size 8 (5mm) needles.
Take time to check gauge.

Note Hat is worked on circular needle to crown, then changes to dpn when there are too few sts to fit comfortably on the circular needle.

EAR FLAPS (make 2)

With 2 dpn and A, cast on 4 sts. Work in garter st for 7"/18cm or approx 70 rows. Bind off. With B, picking up along one long side of A strip, pick up and k 33 sts along one edge of strip, (picking up approx 1 st in every 2 rows).

Next dec row (WS) K14, ssk, k1, k2tog, k14.

Next row K13, k2tog, k1, ssk, k13. Cont to work in garter st and dec in this way every row, having 1 less st before first dec and after 2nd dec, AT SAME TIME, cont in stripe pat of 3 more rows B, 4 rows C, then 6 rows B—3 sts rem.

Next row Sl 2 sts as for k2tog to RH needle without knitting them, k1, pass slipped sts over k st. Cut yarn and pull through rem st.

HAT

With circular needle and D, cast on 19 (21) sts (for back), pick up and k 23 sts from top of one ear flap, cast on 27 (29) sts (for front), pick up and k 23 sts from top of other ear flap—92 (96) sts. Join, taking care not to twist sts on needle. Mark end of rnd and sl marker every rnd. Work 4-st rep of chart 23 (24) times and foll chart through rnd 32.

Dec rnd 33 Foll chart for color, *k2tog, k2; rep from * 22 (23) times more—69 (72) sts.

Rnds 34-38 Work even in chart pat as foll: Work 4-st rep 17 (18) times, work first 1 (0) st once more.

Dec rnd 39 Foll chart for color, *k2tog, k1; rep from * around—46 (48) sts. Cont to foll chart through rnd 50.

Dec rnd 51 *K2tog; rep from * around—23 (24) sts. Cont to foll chart through rnd 55.

Dec rnd 56 *K2tog; rep from *; end k1 (0)—12 sts. Work rnd 57 foll chart.
Dec rnd 58 Cont with B, *k2tog; rep from * around—6 sts. Cont to work in rnds with B on 6 rem sts for 1"/2.5cm (top of hat). Cut yarn and pull through sts on needles. Draw through tightly and fasten off.

FINISHING
Block hat lightly to measurements. With crochet hook and C, working from RS, work an edge of sc around entire hat, including ear flaps, pulling B through last 2 lps of rnd.
Next rnd *Sc in next 2 sc, work sc, ch 2 and sc in next sc (for picot); rep from * around. With C, make two 1½"/4cm twisted cords. With C and D, make two 1"/2.5cm pom-poms and attach to ear flaps with twisted cords.

PERUVIAN CHART

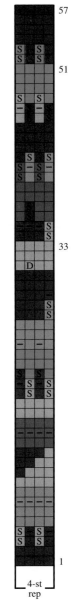

57

51

Color and Stitch key

S Slip st purlwise wyib

— Purl

D Insert RH needle int st 4 rows below
the next st on LH needle, and draw up
a loop; then knit the next st on LH needle
and pass the loop over the st just knitted.

33

Orange (A)

Purple (B)

Teal (C)

Red (D)

Lime (E)

Blue (F)

1

4-st rep

CHENILLE HELMET

Winning modern-day battles

Protect yourself from the elements. Softly structured garter-stitch helmet has a convertible stockinette back flap that ties on top of the head. Designed by Lipp Holmfeld.

SIZES
One size fits Small/Medium or 21-22"/53-56cm

KNITTED MEASUREMENTS
- Head circumference 22"/56cm
- Side depth 3"/7.5cm
- Crown diameter 8"/20.5cm

MATERIALS
- 2 3½oz/100g hanks (each approx 216yd/200m) of Colinette/Unique Kolours *Framework Cotton Chenille* (cotton④) in chestnut
- Size 4 (3.5mm) circular needle, 16"/40cm long *or size to obtain gauge*
- 1 set (5) size 4 (3.5mm) dpn
- Size H/8 (5mm) crochet hook

GAUGES
- 16 sts and 32 rows to 4"/10cm over *St st* using size 4 (3.5mm) needles and single strand of yarn.
- 16 sts and 32 rows to 4"/10cm over *garter st* using size 4 (3.5mm) needles and double strand of yarn.

Take time to check gauges.

BACK FLAP
With single strand of yarn and circular needle, cast on 60 sts. Working back and forth in rows, as with straight needles, k 5 rows.

Next row (WS) K3, p54, k3.

Next row (RS) Knit. Rep last 2 rows until piece measures 3½"/9cm from beg, end with a RS row.

Beg hat
With a double strand of yarn, cast on 24 sts at end of needle (for front of hat), then cont with double strand, k next 30 sts of flap, turn.

Next row Knit all 84 sts, turn. Cont to work back and forth in garter st (so that hat is open at center back) until there are 24 rows or 12 ridges in garter st.

Beg crown
Row 1 (RS) [K11, p1] 7 times. Divide sts evenly over 4 needles (21 sts on each needle). Join, and cont to work in rnds as foll:

Rnd 2 [K2tog, k10] 7 times—77 sts.

Rnd 3 [K10, p1] 7 times.

Rnd 4 [K2tog, k9] 7 times—70 sts.

Rnd 5 [K9, p1] 7 times.

Rnd 6 [K2tog, k8] 7 times—63 sts. Cont to dec in this way every other rnd, having 1 less st after dec on dec rnds and 1 less st before p1 on even rnds until 14 sts rem.

Next rnd *K1, p1; rep from * around.

Next rnd [K2tog] 7 times. P 1 rnd. Cut yarn and pull through all sts on needles twice and draw up tightly to fasten. Secure end inside.

FINISHING
Block lightly to measurements. With double strand of yarn and crochet hook, working from RS into 12th garter ridge of hat, work 1 sc in each st around to form crown

ridge. Join double yarn at garter edge of one side of flap and ch 35 for side tie. Turn, work 1 sc in each ch. Join to hat. Work other side tie in same way.

TASSELED SKI CAP

Hit the slopes!

Tubular-knit alpine cap is worked in a slanting color design. Knit in the round with no shaping, the top corners are tucked in and stitched to form this classic skier's cap. Designed by Susan Mills.

SIZES

Instructions are written for unisex size X-Small (20"/51cm). Changes for sizes Small (21"/53cm), Medium (22"/56cm), Large (23"/59cm) and X-Large (24"/61cm) are in parentheses. Shown in size Small.

KNITTED MEASUREMENTS

▪ Head circumference 18½ (19¼, 20, 20¾, 21½)"/47 (49, 50.5, 52.5, 54.5)cm
▪ Depth 8"/20.5cm

MATERIALS

▪ 1 1¾oz/50g skein each (each approx 110yd/101m) of Reynolds *Paterna* (wool④) in #912 green (A), #707 navy (B), #125 brown (C), #811 wine (D), #957 rust (E) and #439 gold (F)
▪ One each sizes 6 and 8 (4 and 5mm) circular needles, 16"/40cm long *or size to obtain gauge*

GAUGE

21 sts and 24 rows to 4"/10cm over St st and chart pat using larger needle.
Take time to check gauge.

CAP

With smaller needle and A, cast on 97 (101, 105, 109, 113) sts. Join, taking care not to twist sts on needle. Mark end of rnd and sl marker every rnd. K 8 rnds (for St st). P 1 rnd for turning ridge. Change to larger needle

Beg diagonal chart

Rnd 1 Work first st of chart, work 4-st rep 24 (25, 26, 27, 28) times. Work rnds 1-24 twice, then work rnds 1 and 2 once more. With A, bind off all sts.

FINISHING

Fold bound-off edge in half and sew top edge tog so that seam falls to inside. Turn hat inside out and fold and sew top two corners tog in the center. Make 3 multicolored tassels, each 6"/15cm long. Attach to top as in photo.

DIAGONAL CHART

Color key

- Green (A)
- Navy (B)
- Brown (C)
- Wine (D)
- Rust (E)
- Gold (F)

24

20

10

1

4-st
rep

An interlocking Fair Isle diamond pattern in multiples of five demonstrates the refined logic of classic Scottish tam design. The name derives from the eighteenth-century Robert Burns' poem "Tam O' Shanter." Designed by Mari Lynn Patrick.

SIZES
One size fits all.

KNITTED MEASUREMENTS
- Head circumference 22"/56cm
- Diameter 10"/25.5cm

MATERIALS
- 1 1oz/30g hank (each approx 113yd/102m) of Harrisville Designs *Foliage Collection Shetland* (wool①) each in #15 teal (C) and #44 off white (D)
- 1 1½oz/40g hank (each approx 169yd/152m) of Harrisville Designs *Foliage Collection Shetland* (wool①) each in #14 lt teal (A) and #37 brown (B) Yarn is available in kit only. Contact Harrisville Designs for ordering information (1-800-338-9415).
- 1 set (6) each sizes 2 and 4 (2.5 and 3.5mm) dpn *or size to obtain gauge*

GAUGE
28 sts and 28 rows to 4"/10cm over Fair Isle pat st foll chart using larger needles.
Take time to check gauge.

TAM
Beg at band edge, with smaller dpn and A, cast on 150 sts evenly divided onto 5 dpn (30 sts on each needle). Join, taking care not to twist sts on needle. Mark end of rnd and sl marker every rnd. Work in rnds of k1, p1 rib for 2"/5cm. Change to larger dpn.

Next rnd Cont with A, *k9, inc 1 st in next st (by k1 into front and back of st); rep from * 14 times more—165 sts.

Next rnd K4, *inc 1 st in next st, k10; rep from * 14 times more, end last rep k6 instead of k10—180 sts. There are now 36 sts on each of 5 dpn. Then work foll 36-st rep of chart, having 1 complete rep on each dpn, foll rnds 1-25 of chart.

Beg crown decrease
Cut all yarn and reposition the 5 needles to work decreasing at center of each needle as foll: *Needle 1* Sl first 18 sts onto spare needle, sl last 18 sts of rnd (the last 18 sts of 5th needle) to opposite end of spare needle; *Needle 2* Sl first 18 sts of 2nd needle to opposite end of first needle. Cont in this way around repositioning 36 sts onto each of the 5 needles so that each segment is split in half at 18 sts. This way all center line decreases will take place at the center of each dpn, and not in between dpns.

Rnd 26 Rejoin A and B. *Beg with st 19, work sts 19-34 of chart rnd 26 (first 16 sts on needle), then sl next 2 sts as in the position for k2tog (but do not k2tog, only sl to RH needle), k1 with B, pass the 2 sl sts over k st one at a time for 1 double dec, work sts to end of *Needle 1*; rep from * 4 times more. Cont to dec in this way every rnd, working the k1 st before beg dec in color as indicated along left edge of chart, through chart rnd 42. There are 2 sts on each of 5 needles for a total of 10 sts. With D, [k2tog] 5 times. Cut D and pull through rem 5 sts at top twice and fasten securely.

FINISHING

Fold band in half to inside and sew in place. Wash finished hat in lukewarm water and mild soap. Wring out water gently. Insert a 10"/25.5cm plate into hat and allow to dry.

Color key

■ Lt. Teal (A)

▨ Brown (B)

▨ Teal (C)

□ Off White (D)

FAIR ISLE CHART

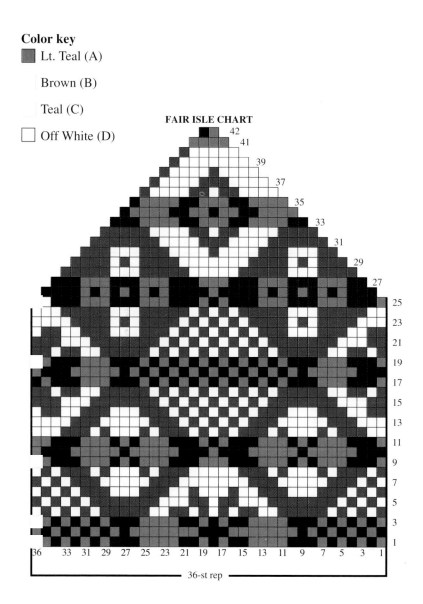

36-st rep

WOOLLY DERBY

Not *for the sheepish*

A soft derby in two versions, one with a folded brim, the other a rolled brim. Soft, nubbly bouclé mimics curly lamb fleece. Designed by Carla Scott.

SIZES
One size fits all.

KNITTED MEASUREMENTS
■ Head circumference 21½"/54.5cm

MATERIALS
Folded brim derby
■ 2 1¾oz/50g balls (each approx 55yd/50m) of Filatura Di Crosa/Stacy Charles Collection *Ariete* (wool/acrylic⑥) in #202 lime green

Rolled brim derby
■ 2 1¾ oz/50g balls (each approx 55yd/50m) of Filatura Di Crosa/Stacy Charles Collection *Ariete* (wool/acrylic⑥) in #209 blue

Note Hats are written for straight knitting with a back seam AND circular knitting with no seam.

Straight version
■ One pair size 8 (5mm) needles *or size to obtain gauge*
■ Small amount of a flat yarn of a matching color for seaming

Circular version
■ One size 8 (5mm) circular needle, 24"/60cm long (for rolled brim only)
■ One size 8 (5mm) circular needle, 16"/40.5cm long *or size to obtain gauge*
■ 1 set (4) size 8 (5mm) dpn

GAUGE
12 sts and 20 rows to 4"/10cm over St st using size 8 (5mm) needles.
Take time to check gauge.

Folded brim—Straight version
With straight needles, cast on 70 sts. Work in St st for 4"/10cm, end with a WS row.
Dec row (RS) [K9, k2tog] 6 times, k4—64 sts. Work even for 4"/10cm more, end with a WS row.

Shape top
Next row (RS) K3, [k2tog, k6] 7 times, k2tog, k3—56 sts. P 1 row.
Next row K2, [k2tog, k5] 7 times, k2tog, k3—48 sts.
Next row P2, [p2tog, p4] 7 times, p2tog, p2—40 sts. K 1 row.
Next row P1, [p2tog, p3] 7 times, p2tog, p2—32 sts.
Next row K1, [k2tog, k2] 7 times, k2tog, k1—24 sts.
Next row [P2tog, p1] 7 times, p2tog, p1—16 sts.
Next row [K2tog] 8 times—8 sts.
Next row [P2tog] 4 times—4 sts.
Fasten off. Pull yarn through sts on needle and draw tog tightly. With flat yarn, sew back seam.

Folded brim—Circular version
With shorter circular needle, cast on 70 sts. Join, taking care not to twist sts on needle. Mark end of rnd and sl marker every rnd. Work in rnds of St st (k every rnd) for 4"/10cm.
Dec rnd [K9, k2tog] 6 times, k4—64 sts. Work even for 4"/10cm more.
Note Change to dpn when there are too few sts to fit on a circular needle.

Shape top

Next rnd K3, [k2tog, k6] 7 times, k2tog, k3—56 sts. K 1 rnd.

Next rnd K2, [k2tog, k5] 7 times, k2tog, k3—48 sts.

Next rnd K2, [k2tog, k4] 7 times, k2tog, k2—40 sts. K 1 rnd.

Next rnd K1, [k2tog, k3] 7 times, k2tog, k2—32 sts.

Next rnd K1, [k2tog, k2] 7 times, k2tog, k1—24 sts.

Next rnd [K2tog, k1] 7 times, k2tog, k1—16 sts.

Next rnd [K2tog] 8 times—8 sts.

Next rnd [K2tog] 4 times—4 sts.

Fasten off. Pull yarn through sts on needle twice and draw up tightly to fasten. Secure end inside

Rolled brim—Straight version

With straight needles, cast on 87 sts. Work in St st for 4"/10cm, end with a WS row.

Next row (RS) K6, [k2tog, k16] 4 times, k2tog, k7—82 sts.

Next row P2, [p2tog, p13] 5 times, p2tog, p3—76 sts.

Next row K2, [k2tog, k12] 5 times, k2tog, k2—70 sts.

Next row P2, [p2tog, p11] 5 times, p2tog, p1—64 sts.

Work even for 4"/10cm more, end with a WS row.

Shape top

Work same as folded brim straight version.

Rolled brim—Circular version

With longer circular needle, cast on 87 sts. Join, taking care not to twist sts on needle. Mark end of rnd and sl marker every rnd. Work in rnds of St st (k every rnd) for 4"/10cm.

Next rnd K6, [k2tog, k16] 4 times, k2tog, k7—82 sts.

Next rnd K2, [k2tog, k13] 5 times, k2tog, k3—76 sts.

Next rnd K2, [k2tog, k12] 5 times, k2tog, k2—70 sts.

Next rnd K2, [k2tog, k11] 5 times, k2tog, k1—64 sts.

Change to shorter circular needle and work even for 4"/10cm more, end with a WS row.

Note Change to dpn when there are too few sts to fit on circular needle.

Shape top

Work same as folded brim circular version.

TASSELED PULL-ON CAP

Explore the mystery of disappearing decreases

Knit flat with a back seam, this cap designed by Wendy Keele is knit in a classic-weight wool yarn. The crown decreases cleverly disappear into the pattern.

SIZES
Instructions are written for Woman's size Small (21"/53cm). Changes for Medium (22"/56cm) and Large (23"/59cm) are in parentheses. Shown in size Small.

KNITTED MEASUREMENTS
▓ Head circumference 20 (21, 22)"/51 (53, 56)cm
▓ Depth 8"/20.5cm

MATERIALS
▓ 1 (1, 2) 3½oz/100g balls (each approx 223yd/204m) of Paton's *Classic Wool* (wool④) in #238 pumpkin
▓ One pair size 7 (4.5mm) needles *or size to obtain gauge*

GAUGE
24 sts and 36 rows to 4"/10cm over pat st using size 7 (4.5mm) needles.
Take time to check gauge.

PATTERN STITCH
(odd number of sts)
Rows 1 and 3 (RS) *K1, p1; rep from *, end k1.
Rows 2 and 4 *P1, k1; rep from *, end p1.
Rows 5-8 Knit.
Rep rows 1-8 for pat st.

CAP
Beg at lower edge and cast on 121 (127, 133) sts. Work in pat st for a total of 6 reps.

Piece measures approx 5½"/14cm from beg. (Adjust length at this point, if desired). Work rows 1-6.
Dec row 7 [K2tog] 60 (62, 66) times, k3tog 0 (1, 0) times, k1 (0, 1)—61 (63, 67) sts.
Row 8 Knit. Work pat rows 1-6.
Dec row 7 [K2tog] 30 (30, 32) times, k3tog 0 (1, 1) time, k1 (0, 0)—31 (31, 33) sts.
Row 8 Knit. Work pat rows 1-6.
Dec row 7 [K2tog] 15 (15, 16) times, k1. Cut yarn leaving long end. Pull yarn through rem 16 (16, 17) sts twice. Draw up lightly and fasten off. Sew back seam.

FINISHING
Lightly steam cap to knitted measurements. Make 2 tassels winding yarn around a 2"/5cm length of cardboard. Secure tassel at top with 3 lengths of yarn, 24"/60cm long. Braid lengths tog to form a 6"/15cm hanging string. Secure tassel by winding one end around at ½"/1.5cm down from top. Attach braided lengths to top of cap. Wind yarn around braids at top of hat several times to secure.

MOSAIC FEZ

Middle Eastern mystery

Named for the Moroccan town of Fez, this hat traditionally sports a single tassel. The dimensional woven look of the all-over mosaic pattern is formed by working one color at a time and slipping the alternate color. Designed by Pam Allen.

SIZES
One size fits all.

KNITTED MEASUREMENTS
▪ Head circumference 21"/53cm
▪ Depth 7½"/19cm

MATERIALS
▪ 1 1¾oz/50g ball (each approx 105yd/96m) of Cleckheaton *Country 8-Ply* by Plymouth (wool④) each in #1083 burgundy (A), #9221 purple (B) and #1644 lt blue (C)
▪ One each sizes 3 and 6 (3 and 4mm) circular needles, 16"/40cm long
▪ One set (4) size 6 (4mm) dpn
▪ Stitch markers

GAUGE
23 sts and 49 rows to 4"/10cm in mosaic pat foll charts using larger needles.
Take time to check gauge.

Notes on mosaic knitting
I To foll the mosaic chart, note that each rnd pictured on the graph represents 2 rnds of knitting (always foll chart from right to left for working in rnds).

2 The first color box to the right of the rnd number represents the working color.
3 On odd (or first) rnds of this color, knit the working color and sl the alternate color wyib. On even (or second) rnds of this color, purl the working color and sl the alternate color wyib.

HAT
Beg at lower edge with smaller circular needle and A, cast on 120 sts. Join, taking care not to twist sts on needle. Mark end of rnd and sl marker every rnd. P every rnd (for rev St st) for 7 rnds. Change to larger circular needle and B.
Next rnd *With tip of RH needle, pick up lp of cast-on st from WS below next st on needle and place on LH needle, k2tog; rep from * around. Band is now rolled under.

Beg chart I
Rnd I Using C, foll chart rnd 1, k all sts in C and sl all sts in B, work 30-st rep 4 times. Cont to foll chart in this way (see notes for mosaic knitting) through rnd 46. Change to smaller circular needle and k 1 rnd with A. P 6 more rnds with A. Change to larger circular needle and B.
Next rnd * With tip of RH needle, pick up lp of A (from WS on first A row) below next st on needle and place on LH needle, k2tog; rep from * around. Rolled edge of brim is completed.
Note When working chart II for crown decs, change to dpn when there are too few sts to fit on circular needle.
Beg chart II
Next rnd *Place marker, with B, ssk, k to st 15 of chart; rep from * 7 times more—112 sts.

Rnd 2 Foll chart, with B, purl.

Rnds 3 and 4 Foll chart, work 14-st rep 8 times. (Be sure to purl sts on even row).

Rnd 5 Sl first marker then, foll chart, *k to within 2 sts of next marker, sl next 2 sts to RH needle without knitting them and drop marker, sl 1 knitwise and insert LH needle into fronts of these 3 sts and k2tog (2-st dec); rep from * around—96 sts. Cont to foll chart in this way, working 2-st dec 8 times (as on rnd 5), on rnds 9, 13, 21, 29, and 37-16 sts rem. Work even foll chart through rnd 41. Cut yarn leaving long end. Pull through sts twice and draw up tightly to fasten. Leave end inside for securing tassel.

FINISHING

Block to measurements. With C, make a 3½"/9cm tassel. Tie tassel at ¾"/2cm from top. Using A, wrap several times around tassel at top. With B, make 5 perpendicular wraps over the wrapped section of tassel in A (see photo) and bring 8"/20.5cm end out of center of tassel. With 2 other A strands, make a braid at top of tassel and attach at top center of hat.

CHART I

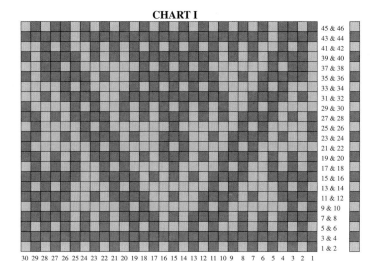

Color key

■ Burgundy (A)

■ Purple (B)

□ Lt blue (C)

⧄ SSK

 sl these 2 sts to
RH needle as for
K2tog without
knitting,
sl1, insert tip of
LH needle into
fronts of these
3 sts and K3tog

CHART II

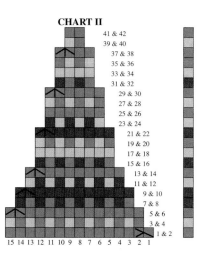

PANSY BERET

How does your garden grow?

Elegant draped beret knit in rich tapestry colors is designed by Sasha Kagan. Tilting pansies on climbing vines are worked in a variety of yarns and encircled by tiny knit-in bobbles.

SIZES
One size fits all.

KNITTED MEASUREMENTS
- Head circumference 23"/59cm
- Depth 10"/25.5cm

MATERIALS
- 1 1¾oz/50g ball (each approx 184yd/170m) of Rowan *True 4-Ply Botany* (wool②) in #563 navy (MC)
- 1 .80oz/25g ball (each approx 72yd/67m) of *Lightweight DK* (wool②) each in #99 purple (A), #611 violet (B), #501 bluebell (C), #423 pale magenta (D) and #14 yellow (I)
- 1 1¾oz/50g ball (each approx 173yd/160m) of *Fine Cotton Chenille* (cotton/polyester③) each in #408 crocus (E) and #410 privet (H)
- 1 .80oz/25g ball (each approx 69yd/64m) of *Kid Silk* (mohair/silk③) each in #992 garnet (F) and #976 opal (G)
- One pair size each sizes 3 and 5 (3 and 3.75mm) needles *or size to obtain gauge*
- 1 set (5) size 5 (3.75mm) dpn
- ¾yd/.70m of 1"/2.5cm wide elastic

GAUGE
32 sts and 34 rows to 4"/10cm over St st and pansy chart using larger needles.
Take time to check gauge.

Note Work each segment of color with a separate ball or bobbin. Carry MC across floral sections but do not carry other colors across back of work.

STITCH GLOSSARY
Make bobble
K1, p1 and k1 into st, turn. K3, turn. P3, turn. K3, turn. P3tog. On next (WS) row, p1 with MC into back lp of bobble st.

BERET
Beg at lower band edge, with smaller needles and MC, cast on 160 sts.
Row 1 *K1, p1; rep from * to end.
Row 2 *P1, k1; rep from * to end. Rep these 2 rows for seed st until piece measures 2½"/6.5cm from beg, end with a RS row.
Next row (WS) Purl, inc 22 sts evenly spaced across—182 sts. Change to larger needles.

Beg pansy chart
Row 1 (RS) Work sts 1-73 of chart twice, then sts 1-36 once. Cont in pat as established through chart row 64.
Next row With MC, purl, dec 6 sts evenly spaced—176 sts.

Crown shaping
Change to dpn and join to work in rnds.
Rnd 1 [K8, SKP] 17 times, K 9—159 sts.
Rnd 2 Knit.

Rnd 3 [K7, SKP] 17 times, K 6—142 sts.
Rnd 4 Knit. Cont to work in this way, dec 17 sts every other rnd, by working 1 less st before decreases, until 57 sts rem.
Next rnd [K2tog] 28 times, k1—29 sts. Cut yarn and pull through sts on needle twice and draw up tightly to fasten. Secure end inside.

Block hat to measurements. Sew back seam. Cut elastic to fit head size and sew to form circle. Fold hem to inside over elastic and sew in place. With A, make a 1½"/4cm pom-pom and sew to top of crown.

Color key

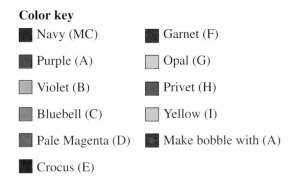

- ⬛ Navy (MC)
- ⬛ Purple (A)
- ⬜ Violet (B)
- ⬛ Bluebell (C)
- ⬛ Pale Magenta (D)
- ⬛ Crocus (E)
- ⬛ Garnet (F)
- ⬜ Opal (G)
- ⬛ Privet (H)
- ⬜ Yellow (I)
- ⬛ Make bobble with (A)

PANSY CHART

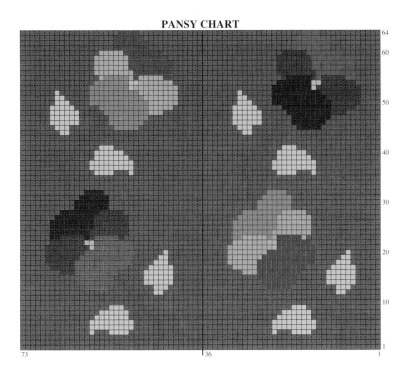

CLOCHE HAT

Always in vogue

Popular in the '20s, then again in the '60s, this double-knit stitch cloche, designed by Mari Lynn Patrick, has a graceful shape. The name derives from the French word for bell.

SIZES

Instructions are written for Woman's size Small (21"/53cm). Changes for sizes Medium (22"/56cm) and Large (23"/59cm) are in parentheses. Shown in size Small.

KNITTED MEASUREMENTS

■ Head circumference 20 (21, 22)"/51 (53, 56)cm
■ Depth 8 (8¼, 8¾)"/20.5 (21, 22)cm

MATERIALS

■ 3 (3, 4) 1¾oz/50g balls (each approx 96yd/86m) of Berroco *Sensu Wool* (wool/nylon④) in #6370 fire red
■ Size 6 (4mm) circular needle, one each 16"/40cm and 24"/60cm long *or size to obtain gauge*
■ 1 set (5) size 6 (4mm) dpn

GAUGE

30 sts and 48 rows to 4"/10cm over double knit st using size 6 (4mm) needles.
Take time to check gauge.

Double Knit Stitch-Straight

(Odd number of sts)
Note This stitch is worked straight for gauge purposes only. Hat is knit entirely in the rnd.

Row 1 (RS) K1, * sl 1 wyib, k1; rep from * to end.
Row 2 K1, *pl, k1; rep from * to end.
Rep rows 1 and 2 for double knit st (straight).

Double Knit Stitch-In the Round

(Even number of sts)
Rnd 1 *K1, sl 1 wyib; rep from * around.
Rnd 2 *P1, k1; rep from * around.
Rep rnds 1 and 2 for double knit st (in the round).

HAT

Beg at brim edge with longer circular needle, cast on 250 (258, 266) sts. Join, taking care not to twist sts on needle. Mark end of rnd and sl marker every rnd. Work in double knit st (in the round) for 11 rnds.
Dec rnd 1 *P3tog (for 2-st dec), work 19 sts in pat; rep from * 10 times more, p3tog, work 5 (13, 21) sts—226 (234, 242) sts. Work even for 5 rnds.
Dec rnd 2 Work 4 (8, 12) sts in pat, *p3tog, work 15 sts in pat; rep from * 11 times more, p3tog, work 3 (7, 11) sts in pat—200 (208, 216) sts. Work even for 5 rnds. Change to shorter circular needle.
Dec rnd 3 K2, [p3tog, work 7 sts in pat] 0 (3, 6) times, [p3tog, work 5 sts in pat] 24 (21, 18) times, p3tog, work 3 (5, 7) sts in pat—150 (158, 166) sts. Work even for 3½ (3¾, 4)"/9 (9.5, 10)cm OR until hat measures 5¼ (5½, 5¾)"/13.5 (14, 14.5)cm from cast-on edge, end with pat rnd 1.

Crown

Change to dpn and divide sts as foll: 37 (39, 41) sts on *Needle 1*; 38 (40, 42) sts on

Needle 2; 37 (39, 41) sts on *Needle 3*; 38 (40, 42) sts on *Needle 4*.

Dec rnd Dec 4 sts on each of 4 dpn (by p3tog for each 2 sts dec'd), spacing decs evenly around—a total of 16 sts dec'd for 134 (142, 150) sts. Rep dec rnd, being sure that decs are spaced so that they don't fall directly on top of each other, every 6th rnd twice more, every 4th rnd twice, every other rnd 3 (3, 4) times—22 (30, 22) sts. Dec 8 sts every other rnd 1 (2, 1) times (2 sts dec'd on each needle)—14 sts rem. K2tog around. Pull yarn through rem 7 sts twice. Draw up tightly and fasten off.

SUMMER STRAW HAT

Sun screen

Cool the summer sizzle with a garter-stitch raffia hat designed by Mari Lynn Patrick. Blocking with starch and a head form is the key to creating a portrait-perfect look.

SIZES

Instructions are for Woman's size Small (21"/53cm). Changes for sizes Medium (22"/56cm) and Large (23"/58.5cm) are in parentheses. Shown in size Medium.

MATERIALS

▓ 4 (5, 5) hanks (each approx 72yd/66m) of Judi & Co. *Raffia* (rayon⑤) in med blue
▓ 1 set (5) size 6 (4mm) dpn *or size to obtain gauge*
▓ Size 6 (4mm) circular needle, 24"/60cm long
▓ One 21 (22, 23)"/53 (56, 58.5)cm head form
▓ Liquid starch (undiluted)
▓ 1yd/1m of 1½"/4cm grosgrain ribbon

GAUGE

16 sts and 32 rows to 4"/10cm over garter st using size 6 (4mm) needles.
Take time to check gauge.

Note Hat is constructed in three steps. First, a band is knit on straight needles to fit around head. After sewing seam, sts are picked up along one edge and crown is worked using dpn. Then sts are picked up along opposite end and brim is worked outwards with circular needle.

BAND

With two size 6 (4mm) dpn, cast on 15 sts. Working back and forth, work in garter st for 172 (180, 188) rows OR until band measures 21 (22, 23)"/53 (56, 58.5)cm long, stretching slightly to fit head. Bind off. Sew cast-on edge to bound-off edge to form circle.

CROWN

With dpn, pick up and k sts along one edge as foll: 20 (21, 22) sts with *Needle 1*, 21 (22, 23) sts with *Needle 2*, 20 (21, 22) sts with *Needle 3* and 21 (22, 23) sts with *Needle 4*—a total of 82 (86, 90) sts. Join and working in garter st rnds, work as foll: k1 rnd, p1 rnd.

Dec rnd Knit, dec 3 sts on each of the 4 needles, spacing decs evenly for a total of 12 sts dec'd. P 1 rnd. Rep last 2 rnds 5 times more—10 (14, 18) sts.

Next rnd [K2tog] 5 (7, 9) times. Pull yarn through rem 5 (7, 9) sts twice. Draw up tightly and fasten off.

BRIM

With dpn, pick up and k 86 (90, 94) sts along opposite edge, dividing sts as foll: 21 (22, 23) sts on *Needles 1 and 3* and 22 (23, 24) sts on *Needles 2 and 4*. K 1 rnd, p 1 rnd.

Inc rnd 1 [K3, inc 1 st in next st] 21 (22, 23) times, k2—107 (112, 117) sts. P 1 rnd, k 1 rnd, p 1 rnd.

Inc rnd 2 [K4, inc 1 st in next st] 21 (22, 23) times, k2—128 (134, 140) sts. Change to circular needle and working back and forth in rows (for back slit), k 3 rows.

Inc row 3 [K5, inc 1 st in next st] 21 (22, 23) times, k2—149 (156, 163) sts. K 1 row.

Inc row 4 [K6, inc 1 st in next st] 21 (22, 23) times, k2—170 (178, 186) sts. K 3 rows.

Inc row 5 [K7, inc 1 st in next st] 21 (22,

23) times, k2—191 (200, 209) sts. K 1 row.
Inc row 6 [K8, inc 1 st in next st] 21 (22, 23) times, k2—212 (222, 232) sts. K 3 rows.
Inc row 7 [K9, inc 1 st in next st] 21 (22, 23) times, k2—233 (244, 255) sts. K 1 row.
Inc row 8 [K10, inc 1 st in next st] 21 (22, 23) times—254 (266, 278) sts. K 3 rows.
Inc row 9 [K11, inc 1 st in next st] 21 (22, 23) times—275 (288, 301) sts. K 2 rows. Bind off knitwise.

FINISHING

To achieve the stiff structure of a classic straw hat, wet-starch blocking with a head form is required.

Fill a basin with enough liquid starch (undiluted) to immerse hat. Gently wring wetness from hat; it will now be very limp. Place hat on head form and stack several books (or other flat objects) around head form in a circle with several pieces of cardboard on top of books to form a flat plane at the brim level. Press head and brim with hands to fit smoothly on form and with brim totally flat. Let dry overnight. Hat shape may be refreshed at any time by spraying with water or steaming while in the same blocking position. Tie ribbon around hat. Form bow; tack in place.

Commedia dell'arte

The six colored wedges that make up the harlequin pattern are worked flat with separate bobbins. A garter-stitch bull's eye with braided tassels completes the crown. Designed by Barbara Venishnick.

SIZES

One size fits all.

KNITTED MEASUREMENTS

- Head circumference 22"/56cm
- Diameter 10"/25.5cm

MATERIALS

- 1 1¾oz/50g ball each (each approx 310yd/283m) of Brown Sheep *Nature Spun Fingering Weight* (wool②) in #N03 grey heather (A), #601 black (B), #N48 scarlet (C), #N62 amethyst (D), #308 gold (E) and #N24 green (F)
- One pair size 4 (3.5mm) needles *or size to obtain gauge*
- ¾yd/.70m of ½"/1.25cm wide gros-grain ribbon
- Bobbins

GAUGE

26 sts and 35 rows to 4"/10cm over St st and pat foll diamond chart using size 4 (3.5mm) needles.
Take time to check gauge.

Notes

1 Wind yarn onto bobbins to work each separate segment of color with a different bobbin (do not carry colors across back of work). Or, if desired, work with separate balls.

2 Work beret back and forth in rows, then sew tog when completed.

BERET

Beg at band edge with A, cast on 149 sts. Beg with a p row, work in St st for 10 rows. K next row on WS for turning ridge. Then working in garter st, k 2 rows B, 2 rows C, 2 rows D, 2 rows E and 2 rows F. K 1 row A.

Next row (WS) With A, *k3, inc 1 st in next st; rep from * 36 times more, k1—186 sts.

Beg diamond chart

Next row (RS) K31 A, k31 B, k31 C, k31 D, k31 E, k31 F. Cont to foll diamond chart in established color sequence through row 6.

Row 7 K15 A, k1 D, k15 A; k15 B, k1 E, k15 B; k15 C, k1 A, k15 C; k15 D, k1 F, k15 D; k15 E, k1 C, k15 E; k15 F, k1 B, k15 F. Cont to foll diamond chart in this way for shaping of diamond and color placement diagram for color sequence in established pat, through row 26.

Row 27 (RS) *K1, ssk, k to last 3 sts of color section, k2tog, k1; rep from * 5 times more—174 sts. Cont to foll diagram for color placement and work decs as on row 27 (12 sts dec'd each dec row) through row 60—54 sts rem. Cut all yarns leaving a 9"/23cm long end of A.

Note For the foll color sequence, leave an end of 7"/18cm for each color.

Next row (RS) With A, [k1, ssk, k3, k2tog, k1] 6 times—42 sts. K 1 row.

Next row (RS) With B, [k1, ssk, k1, k2tog, k1] 6 times—30 sts. K 1 row. With C, k 2 rows.

Next row (RS) With D, [k3, k2tog] 6 times—24 sts. K 1 row.

Next row (RS) With E, [k2, k2tog] 6 times—18 sts. K 1 row.

Next row (RS) With F, [k1, k2tog] 6 times—12 sts. K 1 row.

Next row (RS) With A, [k2tog] 6 times— 6 sts. K 1 row. Pull yarn through sts on needle twice and draw up tightly to fasten. Secure end inside.

FINISHING

Sew invisible side seam using color A. Cut A, leaving a long end. Draw all long ends up through center of beret. Make 5 braids of 3 strands each, as foll: 1 of A and 2 of each of the other colors. Tie a knot at end of each braid and trim ends even. Cut ribbon to 23"/59cm. Overlap ends by 1"/2.5cm and sew tog. Pin ribbon to fit around garter ridge and inside turning ridge at band edge. Fold hem in place and sew over ribbon facing. Neatly finish all ends. Place a 10"/25.5cm diameter plate inside beret and wet block until dry.

Color key

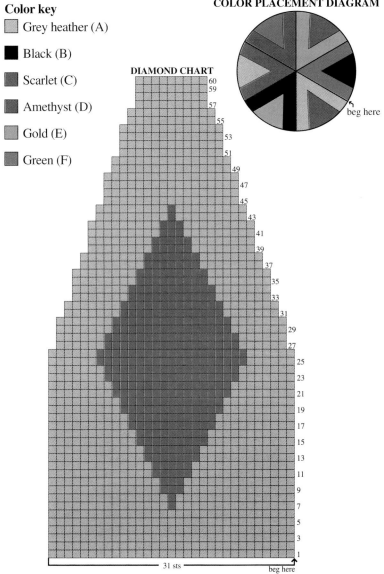

Grey heather (A)

Black (B)

Scarlet (C)

Amethyst (D)

Gold (E)

Green (F)

COLOR PLACEMENT DIAGRAM

beg here

DIAMOND CHART

60
59
57
55
53
51
49
47
45
43
41
39
37
35
33
31
29
27
25
23
21
19
17
15
13
11
9
7
5
3
1

31 sts

beg here

WATCH CAP
Sailor style takes a ribbing

Landlocked or on the high seas, Lila P. Chin's basic beauty chases off winter chills. Easy watch cap worked in 2 x 2 ribbing takes a luxurious turn in sumptuous cashmere.

SIZES
Instructions are written for Unisex sizes X-Small (20"/51cm). Changes for sizes Small/Medium (21-22"/53-56cm) and Large (23"/59cm) are in parentheses. Shown in Woman's size Small/Medium. For children, make size X-Small, for Men make size Large.

KNITTED MEASUREMENTS
▪ Head circumference 17¾ (19½, 21½)"/45 (49.5, 54.5)cm
▪ Depth (folded up) 7½ (8, 8)"/19 (20.5, 20.5)cm

MATERIALS
▪ 1 3½oz/100g hank (each approx 165yd/152m) of Trendsetter Yarns *Dali* (cashmere⑤) in #189 burgundy
▪ 1 set (5) size 8 (5mm) dpn *or size to obtain gauge*

GAUGE
18 sts and 26 rows to 4"/10cm over k2, p2 rib (slightly stretched) using size 8 (5mm) needles.
Take time to check gauge.

CAP
Beg at lower edge, cast on 80 (88, 96) sts evenly divided on 4 needles—20 (22, 24) sts on each needle. Join, taking care not to twist sts on needle. Mark end of rnd and sl marker every rnd.

Rnd 1 *K2, p2; rep from * around. Cont in k2, p2 rib as established until piece measures 8½ (9, 9)"/21.5 (23, 23)cm from beg.
Next rnd *K6, k2tog; rep from * 9 (10, 11) times more—70 (77, 84) sts. K 1 rnd.
Next rnd *K5, k2tog; rep from * 9 (10, 11) times more—60 (66, 72) sts. K 1 rnd.
Next rnd *K4, k2tog; rep from * 9 (10, 11) times more—50 (55, 60) sts. K 1 rnd.
Next rnd *K3, k2tog; rep from * 9 (10, 11) times more—40 (44, 48) sts. K 1 rnd.
Next rnd *K2, k2tog; rep from * 9 (10, 11) times more—30 (33, 36) sts. K 1 rnd.
Next rnd *K1, k2tog; rep from * 9 (10, 11) times more—20 (22, 24) sts. K 1 rnd.
Next rnd *K2tog; rep from * around—10 (11, 12) sts. Cut yarn leaving a long end for sewing. Pull through sts on needles twice and draw up tightly to fasten. Secure end inside.

FINISHING
Lightly block finished cap. Turn cuff up 3"/7.5cm from lower edge and steam lightly in place.

CABLED HAT

The height of fashion

A tall, extended crown lends regal dimensions to Deborah Newton's cabled panel hat. Lush bouncing pom-poms and bright tweedy yarns add to the whimsical look.

KNITTED MEASUREMENTS
- Head circumference 22"/56cm
- Depth 7"/17.5cm

SIZES
One size fits all.

MATERIALS
- 1 3½oz/100g skein each (each approx 196yd/176m) of Classic Elite *London Shetland Wool Tweed* (wool④) in #9045 tangerine (A), #9059 red (B), #9035 lime (C), #9061 fuchsia (D) and #9062 blue (E)
- One pair each sizes 7 and 8 (4.5 and 5mm) needle *or size to obtain gauge*
- One set (5) size 7 (4.5mm) dpn
- Size G/6 (4.5mm) crochet hook
- Cable needle
- St markers
- Bobbins

GAUGE
20 sts and 26 rows to 4"/10cm over cable pat using larger needles.
Take time to check gauge.

STITCH GLOSSARY
2-ST LC
Sl 1 st to cn and hold to *front*, k1, k1 from cn.

2-ST RC
Sl 1 st to cn and hold to *back*, k1, k1 from cn.

4-ST LC
Sl 2 sts to cn and hold to *front*, k2, k2 from cn.

6-ST LC
Sl 3 sts to cn and hold to *front*, k3, k3 from cn.

6-ST RC
Sl 3 sts to cn and hold to *back*, k3, k3 from cn.

MB
(make bobble)
[K into front and back of next st] twice, k into front of st again for 5 sts, turn. P5 turn. K5, turn. P5, turn, SKP, k1, k2tog, turn. P3tog. Bobble is completed.

M1 p-st
With the needle tip, lift the strand between last st worked and the next st on LH needle and purl it.
Note Wind A, B, C and D onto separate bobbins for working side panels.

HAT
With larger needles and A, cast on 23 sts.
Row 1 (WS) P2 (edge sts), k2, p15, k2, p2 (edge sts).
Row 2 (RS) K2 (edge sts), work 19-st panel row 1 foll chart I, k2 (edge sts). Cont to work in this way, keeping 2 edge sts in St st and placing markers every 24th row until 8 rows of chart have been worked 18 times or a total of 144 rows. Piece measures approx 22"/56cm from beg. Bind off.

Side panel
With larger needles, working into first selvage st along one long edge of lower band, pick up and k sts in the foll color sequence: With A, pick up and k 24 sts (1 selvage st and 23 pat sts) to first marker; with B, pick up and k 23 sts to 2nd marker; with A, pick up and k 23 sts to 3rd marker; with D, pick up and k 23 sts to 4th marker; with A, pick up and k 23 sts to 5th

marker; with C, pick up and k 24 sts to end (1 selvage st and 23 pat sts)—140 sts total.

Row I (WS) K1, *p2, k2, p15, k2, p2; rep from * 5 times more, end k1. Cont to work in this way, foll chart I (beg with row 1) for 23-st rep in each color panel (and with k1 selvage sts each end) until row 4 of chart is completed.

Inc row 5 K1, *k2, p1, M1 p st, p1, k15, p1, M1 p st, p1, k2; rep from * 5 times more (12 sts inc'd), end k1—152 sts.

Note Work all inc sts in rev St st. Work even for 3 rows.

Next row (RS) K1, *k2, p1, MB, p1, k15, p3, k2; rep from * 5 times more, end k1. Work 1 row even.

Next row Work 12 M1-p incs as on inc row 5—164 sts. Work in pat for 5 more rows.

Next row Work 12 M1-p incs as on inc row 5—176 sts. Work even until side panel measures 4"/10cm above lower band, end with chart row 2. Bind off in pat.

Crown

Separately, beg at crown center with dpn and E, cast on 8 sts. Divide sts evenly on 4 needles (2 sts on each needle). Join and place marker for end of rnd.

Rnd I K1 tbl in each st.

Rnd 2 K1 into front and back of each st—16 sts.

Rnds 3-5 [K1, p2, k1] 4 times.

Rnd 6 [M1 p-st, k1, M1 k-st, p2, M1 k-st, k1, M1 p st] 4 times—32 sts.

Rnds 7-11 [P1, k2, p2, k2, p1] 4 times.

Rnd 12 [M1 p-st, p1, M1 k-st, k2, M1 k-st and M1 p-st into next strand, p2, M1 p-st and M1 k-st into next strand, k2, M1 k-st, p1, M1 p-st] 4 times—64 sts.

Rnds 13-19 [P2, work chart II over next 4 sts, p4, work chart II over next 4 sts, p2] 4 times.

Rnd 20 *[P1, M1 p-st] twice, work next 4 sts foll chart, [M1 p-st, p1] 4 times, work 4 sts foll chart, [M1 p-st, p1] twice; rep from * 3 times more—96 sts.

Rnds 21-24 [P4, work 4 sts foll chart, p8, work 4 sts foll chart, p4] 4 times.

Rnd 25 *[P2, M1 p-st] twice, work 4 sts foll chart, [M1 p-st, p2] twice, [p2, M1 p-st] twice, work 4 sts foll chat, [M1 p-st , p2] twice; rep from * 3 times more—128 sts.

Rnds 26-28 [P6, work 4 sts foll chart, p12, work 4 sts foll chart, p6] 4 times.

Rnd 29 *Work 3 M1 p-sts evenly over next 6 sts, work 4 sts foll chart, work 6 M1 p-sts evenly over next 12 sts, work 4 sts foll chart, work 3 M1 p sts evenly over next 6 sts; rep from * 3 times more—176 sts.

Rnds 30 and 31 [P9, work 4 sts foll chart, p18, work 4 sts foll chart, p9] 4 times.

Trim edge—last rnd

Turn work so that WS of crown is facing. Working with A, cast on 3 sts on end of needle. Then with spare dpn, *k2, ssk the A st with next E st on needle*, then sl 3 sts back to LH needle and rep between *'s until all sts in E are worked with corded trim in A. Fasten off.

FINISHING

Block pieces to measurements. Sew cast-on edge of lower cable band to bound-off edge to form tube. Steam crown lightly, working with fingers to shape flat. Sew lower cable band to crown underneath corded trim edge. Turn lower edge of band to inside along edge of cable and with double strand A, sew down hem using running stitch, leaving ends free. Tie ends tightly (or loosely) to fit head snugly at band edge.

Crochet cords

With crochet hook and B, ch 5"/12.5cm, sl st in each ch and fasten off. With C, ch 6"/15cm and work in same way. With D, ch 8"/20.5cm, and work in same way.

Pom-poms

Make one (1½"/4cm in size) pom-pom each in colors A, B, C and D. Attach B, C and D pom-poms to same colored cords. Attach cords and A pom-pom to crown (see photo).

CHART I

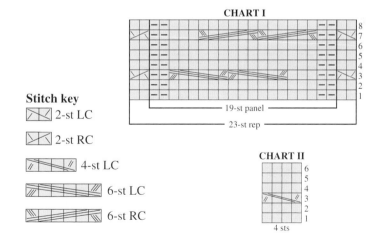

19-st panel

23-st rep

Stitch key

⬜ 2-st LC

⬜ 2-st RC

⬜ 4-st LC

⬜ 6-st LC

⬜ 6-st RC

CHART II

6
5
4
3
2
1

4 sts

A field and stream classic, reinterpreted by Teva Durham. The brim is backed with fused fabric, then top-stitched by hand or machine. A buckled band and knit-in eyelets complete the picture.

SIZES

Instructions are written for Woman's size X-Small (20"/51cm). Changes for size Small/Medium (21-22"/53-56cm) are in parentheses. Shown in size X-Small.

KNITTED MEASUREMENTS

- Head circumference 21½ (22½)"/54.5 (57cm)
- Brim 2¾"/7cm

MATERIALS

- 2 1¾oz/50g balls (each approx 126yd/117m) of GGH/Muench Yarns *Baluga* (cotton③) in #81 lime
- Size 3 (3mm) circular needle, 24"/60cm long *or size to obtain gauge*
- One set (5) size 3 (3mm) dpn
- Stitch marker
- ½yd/.5m of cotton fabric (for lining brim)
- Paper-backed fusible web
- Thread to match
- 1yd/.95m of milliner's petersham or grosgrain ribbon (for band)
- Four size ¾"/20mm brass "D" rings

GAUGE

24 sts and 30 rows to 4"/10cm over St st using size 3 (3mm) needles.
Take time to check gauge.

HAT

Brim

With circular needle, cast on 200 (208) sts. Join, taking care not to twist sts on needle. Mark end of rnd and sl marker every rnd. K 3 rnds.

Next dec rnd *K2tog, k14 (15), [k2tog, k10] twice, k2tog, k14 (15), [k2tog, k20 (21)] twice; rep from * once—188 (196) sts. K 3 rnds.

Next dec rnd *K2tog, k13 (14), [k2tog, k9] twice, k2tog, k13 (14), [k2tog, k19 (20)] twice; rep from * once—176 (184) sts. K 3 rnds.

Next dec rnd *K2tog, k 12 (13), [k2tog, k8] twice, k2tog, k12 (13), [k2tog, k18 (19)] twice; rep from * once—164 (172) sts. K 3 rnds.

Note Change to dpn when there are too few sts to fit on circular needle.

Next dec rnd *K2tog, k11 (12), [k2tog, k7] twice, k2tog, k11 (12), [k2tog, k17 (18)] twice; rep from * once—152 (160) sts. K 3 rnds.

Next dec rnd *K2tog, k10 (11), [k2tog, k6] twice, k2tog, k10 (11), [k2tog, k16 (17)] twice; rep from * once—140 (148) sts. K 3 rnds.

Next dec rnd *K2tog, k9 (10), [k2tog, k5] twice, k2tog, k9 (10), [k2tog, k15 (16)] twice; rep from * once—128 (136) sts.

Band

P 1 rnd.

Next rnd K48 (50), p1 (side "seam"), k63 (67), p1 (side "seam"), k15 (17). Keeping p sts for side "seams" as established, work 5 more rnds. Then, p 1 rnd on all sts.

Sides

Cont with p1 side "seams", work even in St st for 11 rnds.

Next rnd *Work to 10 sts before first p st, k2tog, yo (for eyelet), work to 10 sts after p st, k2tog, yo; rep from * once, k to end. Work even in St st for 11 rnds. P 1 rnd.

Crown

Next dec rnd [K2tog, k4 (3)] 8 (10) times, [k4 (3), k2tog] 10 (12) times, k4 (1), [k4 (2), k2tog] 2 (6) times, k4 (1)—108 sts. Cut yarn and reposition sts onto 5 dpn AND circular needle as foll: Starting at beg of rnd, sl 5 sts to *dpn 1*; 17 sts to circular needle; 9 sts to *dpn 2*; 28 sts to *dpn 3*; 17 sts to *dpn 4*; 28 sts to *dpn 5*; sl last 4 sts to other end of dpn 1. Beg with sts on circular needle, reattach yarn and working with circular needle, k17, turn. P17 from circular needle and p 1 st from *Needle 1*, turn. K18 sts from circular needle and k1 st from *Needle 2*, turn. P19 sts from circular needle and p 1 st from *Needle 1*, turn. K20 sts from circular needle and k 1 st from *Needle 2*, turn. Cont in this way until there are 35 sts on circular needle and 0 sts on *Needles 1 and 2*.

Next row (WS) P34, sl next st to *Needle 5* and p2tog from *Needle 5*, turn.

Next row (RS) K34, sl next st to *Needle 3* and p2tog from *Needle 3*, turn. Rep last 2 rows until 9 sts rem on *Needle 3* and 9 sts on *Needle 5*.

Next row (WS) P to last 2 sts on circular needle and sl these 2 sts to *Needle 5*, p3tog from *Needle 5*, turn.

Next row (RS) K to last 2 sts on circular needle and sl these 2 sts to *Needle 3*, p3tog from *Needle 3*, turn. Rep these 2 rows until 17 sts rem on circular needle and 0 sts rem on *Needles 3* and *5*. P 1 row. With tapestry needle, weave rem 17 sts tog with 17 sts from *Needle 4* using Kitchener st.

Band straps

(make 2)

Cast on 7 sts. Work in k1, p1 rib for 2"/5cm. Dec 1 st each side every other row twice. K3tog. Fasten off.

FINISHING

Block hat to lie flat. Place hat on top of paper side of iron-on fusible web and trace the brim outline. Press cotton fabric and lay out on flat surface, WS facing. Place fusible web diagonally on top of fabric. Following manufacturer's instructions, iron, but do not peel off paper backing. Cut along brim line. Fold in two and carefully cut out center (this piece will fit the crown center). Try hat on and adjust to fit, cutting small snips in fabric around corners for flexibility. Peel off paper backing. Place hat on ironing board with WS of brim facing. Pull crown free so that brim is flat. Place fabric with fusible side down onto brim, matching edges. Press fabric with iron, then press again from RS. Topstitch, by machine or hand, around brim at ½"/1.25cm intervals (or along dec rnds of hat). Repeat fusing process with hat crown (but do not topstitch). Cut ribbon or petersham to fit band, plus 1½"/4cm. Fold under ¾"/2cm at each short end and tack to inside of hat. Try on again to be sure hat is not too tight. Sew lower edge of band to band of hat (leave top edge free). Sew strap to outside of hat (see photo). Sew 2 D-rings opposite with several strands of yarn. Adjust hat with straps.

JESTER'S CAP
Just fooling around

For Intermediate Knitters

A hat with a sense of humor, designed by Nicky Epstein, features bi-color ribbing and stuffed cones affixed to tri-color wedges. Pom-poms replace the traditional bells.

SIZES
Instructions are written for Child's or Adult's size Small/Medium (21-22"/51-53cm).

KNITTED MEASUREMENTS
- Head circumference 18¼"/46.5cm
- Depth (excluding points) 6"/15cm

MATERIALS
- 1 3½/100g ball each (each approx 215yd/195m) of Lane Borgosesia *Knitaly®* (wool④) in #3657 lt green (A), #410 lt blue (B) and #90424 lilac (C)
- One pair each sizes 5 and 6 (3.75 and 4mm) needles *or size to obtain gauge*
- Polyester fiberfill (for stuffing)
- Bobbins

GAUGE
21 sts and 26 rows to 4"/10cm over St st using larger needles.
Take time to check gauge.

HAT
Beg at lower band edge, with smaller needles and B, cast on 98 sts.
Note When working ribbing, carry yarn not in use loosely across back of work.

Row 1 (RS) K1 (selvage st) *K3 A, P3 B; rep from *, end k1 (selvage st).
Row 2 K1, *K3 B, p3 A; rep from *, end k1. Rep these 2 rows until piece measures 1½"/4cm from beg, end with a WS row. Change to larger needles and k 2 rows with C.

Beg crown pat
Note Work each segment of color with a separate ball or bobbin, do not carry yarn across back of work.

Next row (RS) K1 (selvage st), *K16 C, k16 B, k16 A; rep from * once, end k1 (selvage st). Cont in St st in established colors until piece measures 2"/5cm above garter ridge in C, end with a WS row.
Next row (RS) K1, *ssk, k12, k2tog; rep from * 5 times more, k1—86 sts. P 1 row.
Next row K1, *ssk, k10, k2tog; rep from * 5 times more, k1—74 sts. P 1 row.
Next row K1, *ssk, k8, k2tog; rep from * 5 times more, k1—62 sts. P 1 row.
Next row K1, *ssk, k6, k2tog; rep from * 5 times more, k1—50 sts. P 1 row.
Next row K1, *ssk, k4, k2tog; rep from * 5 times more, k1—38 sts. P 1 row.
Next row K1, *ssk, k2, k2tog; rep from * 5 times more, k1—26 sts. P 1 row.
Next row [K2tog] 13 times—13 sts. Cut yarn and pull through sts on needle twice and draw up tightly to fasten. Leave end for sewing back seam later.

Points
Make 2 each in A, B and C.
With larger needles and A, B or C, cast on 19 sts. Work in St st for 2"/5cm.
Next row (RS) K1, ssk, k13, k2tog, k1. P1 row.

Next row K1, ssk, k to last 3 sts, k2tog, k1. P 1 row. Rep last 2 rows until 5 sts rem on last dec row. P 1 row.

Next row K1, SK2P, k1. P3tog. Cut yarn and pull through sts on needle twice and draw up tightly to fasten. Leave end for sewing seam.

Block pieces. Sew seams of each point. Make six 2"/5cm pom-poms (2 in each color) and sew to point (see photo). Stuff points and affix cast-on edges to hat (see photo). Sew back seam of hat.

AFGHANI CAP

Urban legend

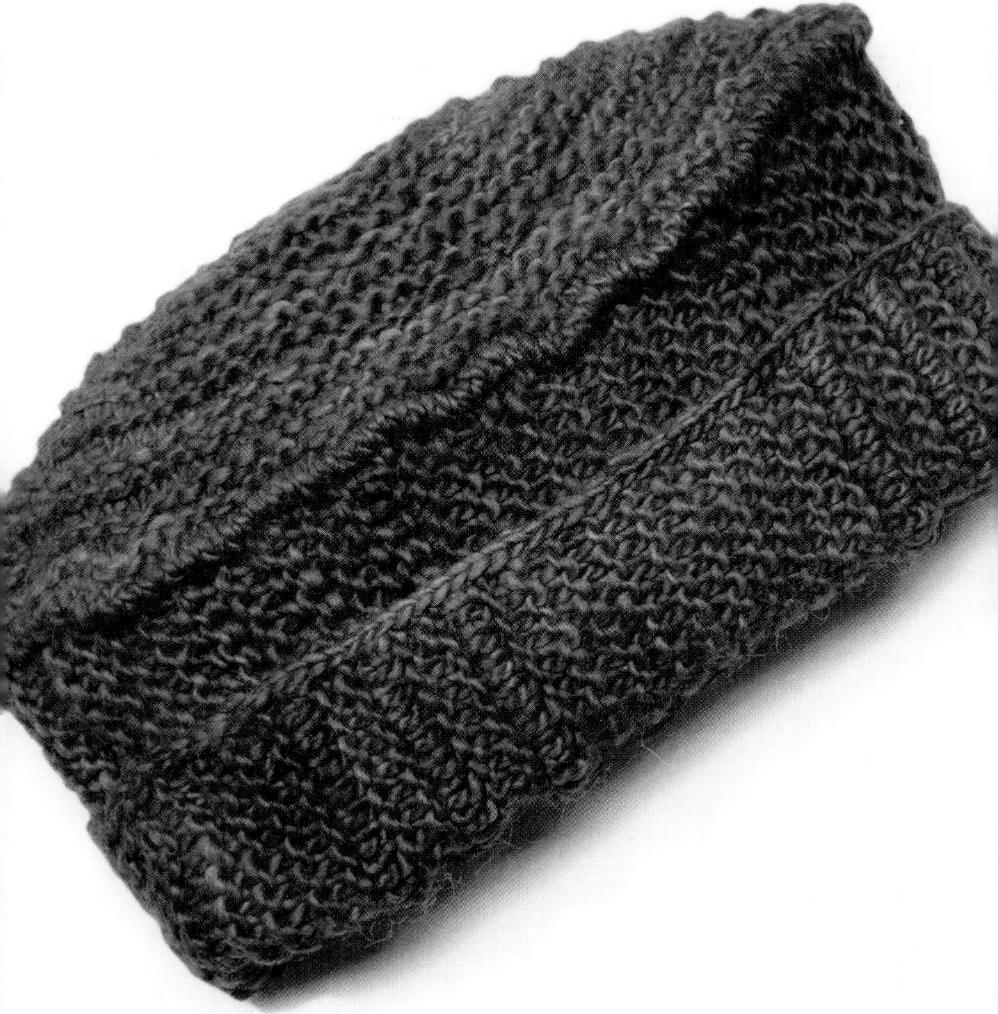

This knitted version of the traditional felt style is designed by Teva Durham. The welted brim is knit straight; the crown is then worked along one side.

SIZES

Instructions are written for Unisex size Small/Medium (21-22")/51-53cm). Changes for size Large/X-Large (23-24"/59-61cm) are in parentheses. Shown in size Large/X-Large.

KNITTED MEASUREMENTS

■ Head circumference 20 (23)"/50.5 (58.5cm)
■ Depth 4"/10cm

MATERIALS

■ 2 3½oz/100g hanks (each approx 137yds/127m) of Manos del Uruguay/Simpson Southwick *700 Tex* (wool④) in #I
■ Size 9 (5.5mm) needles *or size to obtain gauge*
■ Crochet hook size E/4 (3.5mm)

GAUGE

14 sts and 22 rows to 4"/10cm over garter st using size 9 (5.5mm) needles.
Take time to check gauge.

STITCHES USED

Welt Stitch

Row 1 (RS) Tie yarn marker (or secure safety pin) into 1st st and last st on needle, knit across row.
Rows 2-4 Work in St st.
Row 5 With RH needle, in back of work, pick up first st 4 rows below (marked row) and k this st tog with next st on LH needle, cont in this way across row, using markers as guidelines so that you work straight across back of sts on row 1.

BRIM

Cast on 22 sts. Work in garter st for 2½"/6cm, end with a WS row. *Work 5 rows welt st. Work 3 rows garter st. Work 5 rows welt st. Work 3 rows garter st. Work 5 rows welt st. Work in garter st for 3½"/9cm. Rep from * until piece measures 20 (23)"/50.5 (58.5cm). Bind off.

TOP

With WS facing, pick up and k 108 (126) sts along one long side of edge of brim. Work 5 rows welt st.
Next row (WS) K2, *k2tog, k4; rep from *, end k2tog, k2—90 (105) sts. K 1 row.
Next row K2, *k2tog, k3; rep from *, end k2tog, k1—72 (84) sts. K 3 rows.
Next row K1, *k2tog, k2; rep from *, end k2tog, k1—54 (63) sts. K 5 rows.
Next row *K2tog, k1; rep from * to end—36 (42) sts. K 5 rows.
Next row K2tog across row—18 (21) sts. K 1 row.
Next row *K2tog; rep from * to last 0 (3) sts, k0 (3) tog—9 (10) sts. K 1 row.
Next row K2tog across row, end k1 (0)—5 sts. Run yarn through sts on needle twice and secure.

FINISHING

Block gently. Sew back seam from center top down. With RS facing and crochet hook, work 1 rnd sc around edge of brim. Fold up brim.

BASKETWEAVE CAP

Straight off the runway

Merino basketweave sides are topped with a lush angora and merino crown. Sides are lined with ribbing for extra warmth and snug fit. This sumptuous designer original comes from the Fall '98 Joan Vass Collection.

SIZES
One size fits all.

KNITTED MEASUREMENTS
■ Head circumference 18"/45.5cm
■ Depth 6"/15.5cm

MATERIALS
■ 2 1¾oz/50g balls (each approx 121yd/110m) of Baruffa/Lane Borgosesia *Maratona®* (wool④) in ecru #1205 (A)
■ 2 .40oz/10g (each approx 35yd/32m) of Filatura Di Crosa/Stacy Charles Collection *Angorissima* (angora/lambswool④) in #104 ecru (B)
■ One pair size 10½ (6.5mm) dpn *or size to obtain gauge*

GAUGE
16 sts and 26 rows to 4"/10cm over basketweave st using size 10½ (6.5mm) needles. *Take time to check gauge.*

STITCH GLOSSARY
Basketweave Stitch
(multiple of 6 sts)

Rnds 1 and 5 Knit.
Rnds 2-4 K1, *p4, k2; rep from *, end p4, k1.
Rnds 6-8 P2, *k2, p4; rep from *, end k2, p2.
Rep rnds 1-8 for basketweave st.

HAT
With A, cast on 72 sts. Join, taking care not to twist sts on needle. Mark end of rnd and sl marker every rnd. Work in k1, p1 rib for 5½"/14cm. Working with one strand A and B held tog, p 2 rnds for turning ridge. Drop B. Work in basketweave st for 5½"/14cm, end with rnd 4 or 8. K 1 rnd. Working with one strand of A and B held tog, p 6 rnds. K 1 rnd.
Dec rnd [K2tog, k7] 8 times—64 sts. K 1 rnd. Cont to dec 8 sts every other rnd, with one less k st between decs, until 8 sts rem. Cut yarn and pull through sts on needle twice and draw up tightly to fasten. Secure end inside. Fold rib section of hat to WS at turning ridge and sew in place.

NOTES

NOTES

RESOURCES

Write to the yarn companies listed below for purchasing and mail-order information.

BARUFFA
distributed by Lane Borgosesia

BERROCO, INC.
14 Elmdale Road
PO Box 367
Uxbridge, MA 01569

BROWN SHEEP CO., INC.
100662 County Road 16
Mitchell, NE 69357

CARAVAN BEADS
449 Forrest Avenue
Portland, ME 04101
(207) 761-2503
(800) 230-8941
e-mail: info@caravanbeads.com
www.caravanbeads.com

CLASSIC ELITE YARNS, INC.
12 Perkins Street
Lowell, MA 01854

CLECKHEATON
distributed by Plymouth Yarn

COATS PATONS
1001 Roselawn Avenue
Toronto, ON M6B 1B8
Canada

COLINETTE YARN, LTD.
distributed by
Unique Kolours, Ltd.

DALE OF NORWAY, INC.
N16 W23390 Stoneridge Drive
Suite A
Waukesha, WI 53188

FILATURA DI CROSA
distributed by
Stacy Charles Collection

GGH
distributed by Muench Yarns

GRIGNASCO
distributed by JCA

HARRISVILLE DESIGNS
Center Village
Box 806
Harrisville, NH 03450

JCA
35 Scales Lane
Townsend, MA 01469

JUDI & CO.
18 Gallatin Drive
Dix Hills, NY 11746

KOIGU WOOL DESIGNS
R.R. #1
Williamsford, ON N0H 2V0
Canada

LANE BORGOSESIA
PO Box 217
Colorado Springs, CO 80903

LION BRAND YARNS
34 West 15th Street
New York, NY 10011
www.lionbrand.com

MANOS DEL URUGUAY
distributed by
Simpson Southwick Co.

MUENCH YARNS
285 Bel Marin Keys
Boulevard #J
Novato, CA 94949

PLYMOUTH YARN
PO Box 28
Bristol, PA 19007

REYNOLDS
distributed by JCA

ROWAN
distributed by
Westminster Fibers

SIMPSON SOUTHWICK CO.
55 Curtiss Place
Maplewood, NJ 07040

STACY CHARLES COLLECTION
1059/1061 Manhattan Avenue
Brooklyn, NY 11222

TAHKI IMPORTS, LTD.
11 Graphic Place
Moonachie, NJ 07074

TRENDSETTER YARNS
16742 Stagg Street
Suite 104
Van Nuys, CA 91406

UNIQUE KOLOURS, LTD.
1428 Oak Lane
Downingtown, PA 19335

WESTMINSTER FIBERS
5 Northern Boulevard
Amherst, NH 03031

*Write to US resources for
mail-order availability
of yarns not listed.*

BERROCO, INC.
distributed by
R. Stein Yarn Corp.

**CLASSIC ELITE YARNS,
INC.**
distributed by
S. R. Kertzer, Ltd.

CLECKHEATON
distributed by Diamond Yarn

COATS PATONS
1001 Roselawn Avenue
Toronto, ON M6B 1B8

COLINETTE YARNS
distributed by Diamond Yarn

DIAMOND YARN
9697 St. Laurent
Montreal, PQ H3L 2N1 and
1450 Lodestar Road
Unit #4
Toronto, ON M3J 3C1

**ESTELLE DESIGNS &
SALES, LTD.**
Units 65/67
2220 Midland Avenue
Scarborough, ON M1P 3E6

FILATURA DI CROSA
distributed by Diamond Yarn

GRIGNASCO
distributed by
Estelle Designs & Sales, Ltd.

S. R. KERTZER, LTD.
105A Winges Road
Woodbridge, ON L4L 6C2

KOIGU WOOL DESIGNS
R.R. #1
Williamsford, ON N0H 2V0

PATONS
distributed by Coats Patons

R. STEIN YARN CORP.
5800 St-Denis
Suite 303
Montreal, PQ H2S 3L5

ROWAN
distributed by
Diamond Yarn

TAHKI IMPORTS, LTD.
distributed by
Estelle Designs & Sales, Ltd.

---

*Not all yarns used in this
book are available in
the UK. For yarns not
available, make a
comparable substitute or
contact the US manufacturer
for purchasing and
mail-order information.*

COATS CRAFTS UK
distributors of Patons
PO Box 22
The Lingfield Estate
Darlington
Co. Durham DL1 1YQ
Tel: 01325-365457

*In the UK, Cleckheaton is
sold as Jarol Super Saver DK*
JAROL, LTD.
White Rose Mills
Cape Street
Canal Road
Bradford, BD1 4RN
Tel: 01274-392274

COLINETTE YARNS, LTD.
Units 2-5
Banwy Industrial Estate
Llanfair Caereinion
Powys SY21 OSG
Tel: 02938-810128

KILCARRA YARN, LTD.
distributors of Donegal Tweed
Kilcar
Co. Donegal
Ireland
Tel: 00-353-73-38055

ROWAN YARNS
Green Lane Mill
Holmfirth
West Yorks HD7 1RW
Tel: 01484-681881

VOGUE KNITTING CAPS & HATS

Editor-in-Chief
TRISHA MALCOLM

Art Director, Butterick® Company, Inc
JOE VIOR

Book Designer
CHRISTINE LIPERT

Senior Editor
CARLA S. SCOTT

Managing Editor
DARYL BROWER

Instruction Editor
MARI LYNN PATRICK

Knitting Coordinator
JEAN GUIRGUIS

Yarn Coordinator
VERONICA MANNO

Charts & Schematics Illustrator/
Page Layout
ELIZABETH BERRY

Instructions Coordinator
CHARLOTTE PARRY

Editorial Coordinator
KATHLEEN KELLY

Photography
BRIAN KRAUS, NYC
Photographed at Butterick Studios

Project Director
CAROLINE POLITI

Production Managers
LILLIAN ESPOSITO
WINNIE HINISH

Publishing Consultant
MIKE SHATZKIN, THE IDEALOGICAL COMPANY

President and CEO, Butterick® Company, Inc
JAY H. STEIN

Executive Vice President and Publisher, Butterick® Company, Inc
ART JOINNIDES